1 0 0
Favorite
Flowering
Shrubs

100
Favorite
Flowering
Shrubs

PAT KITE

MetroBooks

DEDICATION

To Nancy Neely, teacher, whose enthusiasm so long ago

encouraged my lifetime interest in science.

MetroBooks

An Imprint of Friedman/Fairfax Publishers

©1999 by Michael Friedman Publishing Group, Inc.

Library of Congress Cataloging-in-Publication Data available upon request.

ISBN 1-56799-699-X

Editor: Susan Lauzau
Art Director: Jeff Batzli
Layout Designer: Meredith Miller
Photography Editor: Valerie E. Kennedy
Production Manager: Niall Brennan

Color separations by Ocean Graphic International Company Ltd.
Printed in Singapore by KHL Printing Co Pte Ltd.

1 3 5 7 9 10 8 6 4 2

For bulk purchases and special sales, please contact:
Friedman/Fairfax Publishers
Attention: Sales Department
15 West 26th Street
New York, NY 10010
212/685-6610   FAX 212/685-1307

Visit our website:
http://www.metrobooks.com

Photography credits:

CONTENTS

Introduction

Flowering shrubs play an ever-increasing role in today's landscapes, whether you garden on a large country estate, a suburban yard, a compact patio space, or even a balcony. Plant suppliers and professional hybridizers are working continuously to provide a plant for every niche, from the tiniest woody shrub to a towering vision. Shrubs offer a diversity of seasonal color, shelter for wild animals, food for birds, pollen for honeybees, and fresh and dried flowers for home decoration. They help conceal unattractive areas, and represent a friendly way to mark boundary lines; dense and thorny hedges can even be used to deter trespassers. Shrubs, like other plants, are also essential in creating a clean living environment for all creatures roaming the earth.

WHAT IS A SHRUB?

Confusion exists about the difference between a shrub and a tree. Shrubs usually have several woody stems that branch from the base; rather than a main trunk, like trees, shrubs have multiple branches at the base. Also, shrubs—ranging in size from about 8 inches (20cm) to 15 feet (4.5m) tall—are generally shorter than trees. There are borderline species, however, sometimes called "treelike shrubs" or "shrublike trees," which may grow taller. Some species may

be pruned to a single trunk like a tree or let alone to develop the characteristic shrublike branching stem. With today's less spacious garden sites, a shrub trained as a small tree may be ideal for your garden.

Each entry denotes the plant size, but because so many new cultivars and varieties are available today, make sure to check with the nursery about the ultimate size of the specific plant you are purchasing. This is especially important if you need a shrub of a specific height or width.

Time to Plant

Deciduous shrubs, those that lose their leaves in autumn, should be planted after leaf fall and before spring leaf appearance. In general, shrubs planted in early to mid-autumn make better new growth and produce more flowers than shrubs planted in spring. Winter planting is impossible in areas that receive snow, since frost in the soil will cause the shrub to wilt and die, but many warm-winter regions allow for easy winter planting.

Evergreen shrubs are best planted in early spring, late summer, or early autumn. While planting can be done in late autumn, the shrub doesn't have time to get established before growth ceases for the winter.

Purchasing Shrubs

Deciduous shrubs are often sold bareroot, that is, loosely surrounded by some type of biodegradable packing material. Later in the season, shrubs may appear in earth-filled containers, which somewhat increases the cost.

Evergreen shrubs should not be purchased bareroot, but rather should be "balled and burlapped" (B&B), which means that their roots are surrounded by soil, then tightly wrapped in burlap or other protective material. In many garden shops, evergreens are always sold in containers. Shrubs purchased through the mail are nearly always sold bareroot, as shipping the relatively heavy soil necessary for containerized or B & B plants adds much to the cost of the shrub.

Planting

While preparing the planting hole, newly purchased shrubs should be kept in a wind-free, shaded area. Some people like to soak the plant roots of both bareroot and containerized plants before planting. All wrapping materials should be removed immediately before planting. Metal containers should be cut away without damaging plant roots. You can ask the nursery to do this for you. Some small shrubs are now available in biodegradable containers that may be placed directly into the ground. One important caution: do not let plants in a container dry out in the interim between purchase and planting.

Dig a hole at least 12 inches (30cm) deeper and wider than the estimated root spread. Place at least 8 inches (20 cm) of good topsoil nearby. If this is not available in your garden, purchase it in advance of planting. Putting a shrub in nutritionally deficient, rocky, salty, or otherwise incompatible soil is dooming it to slow growth or possible death. Those shrubs that do well in difficult soil situations are specifically noted in the text.

Place a layer of topsoil at the bottom of the planting hole and firm it down. Gently spread the roots out on this topsoil layer. Put topsoil over the roots a little at a time, firming down each layer. When the hole is two-thirds full, add water. This eliminates small air pockets and provides moisture for the roots.

After the water has settled, fill the planting hole with soil to about an inch below regular ground level. This small basin helps prevent water runoff. Use good organic soil as the remaining backfill whenever possible, although ordinary garden soil will suffice. When finished, the shrub base should be at about the same level as it was in the nursery. You can determine this by noting the bark discoloration at its base. Most shrubs do not need staking. If you chose to stake your shrub, place the stake firmly in the hole before planting the shrub.

PLANTING TIPS

The following hints will help you purchase and care for your new shrubs properly:

• Do not purchase shrubs that have visible girdling roots or shrubs that have become rootbound (the roots have completely filled the container and are pushing out the container holes). It is difficult for these roots to grow correctly into the soil and they dry out easily.

• Shrubs planted in the vicinity of the wide-spreading, shallow roots of such trees as maple, chestnut, birch, and alder may fail to thrive because the trees extract much of the water and nutrients from the soil.

• Under deep-rooted trees such as pine, larch, ash, and oak, make certain to plant shrubs that do well in shade.

• If you are growing shrubs in decorative pots, always use pots with drainage holes. Soggy soil will kill a plant quickly.

• In difficult planting areas, or if you prefer not to spend a lot of time in the garden, use native plants. There may be a native plant society in your area that can advise you about the best choices for your region, or you can find information at the local library.

• Shrubs chosen because of their colorful flowers or berries are more effective in groups of three, five, or seven.

CARE AND MAINTENANCE

It is extremely important that you water the shrub thoroughly around its entire root area for the first few days after planting, and every few days thereafter until the leaves no longer wilt. The existing roots of a newly planted shrub are not immediately capable of moving into the soil for water, and they will die if deprived. After the initial settling-in period, you may water less frequently, according to the plant's needs as noted in its description. However, even shrubs touted as drought-tolerant must be watered initially so that the soil does not dry out. Drought-tolerant shrubs must first develop a sturdy root system, and this takes at least one season. About 4 inches (10cm) of mulch around the base of newly planted shrubs reduces water evaporation and keeps down weeds.

Some shrubs need or benefit from regular pruning, and these species are noted in the individual entries. All shrubs should be checked periodically for dead and decaying branches, and these branches should be removed before decay has a chance to spread to other parts of the shrub.

PESTS AND DISEASES

Common-sense care diminishes possible pest and disease problems. Wise shrub selection, proper light, adequate water, good soil, shelter from the elements where necessary, and regular fertilizer allow plants to resist many pest depredations. Do not purchase sickly looking plants. Watch out for discolored or spotty leaves, tiny bumps on trunk or branches, wilting leaves, and, of course, visible insects of any kind that appear to be feasting on the plant. Common sap-feeding insects include aphids, scale, thrips, and whiteflies. Minute mites are especially attracted to water-stressed and dusty plants. Try hosing tiny pests off or use an insecticidal soap spray.

Abelia grandiflora

Glossy abelia

BLOOM TIME: summer–autumn

HEIGHT/WIDTH: 6' × 5' (1.8 × 1.5m)

LIGHT: full sun–partial shade

ZONES: 6–9

OTHER: attracts butterflies, honeybees

Glossy abelia

This vigorous abelia provides tubular flowers in white to soft lilac-pink from June through first frost. The delicate flowers cluster at branch ends. A stunning cultivar called 'Edward Goucher' has dark green leaves that turn bronze to purplish in autumn and winter. The compact 'Frances Mason' has variegated foliage, while 'Golden Glow' has leaves of sunny yellow.

In mild climates, the shrub's small, glossy leaves are retained throughout the year, though it will drop its leaves in cooler regions. In all climates, shelter glossy abelia from wind. Often planted for its graceful, arching branches, a pleasing shape is achieved through precise pruning in winter and early spring. Even when winters are not that severe, expect some winterkill and be sure to remove deadwood in early spring. Abelia prefers well-drained acidic soil, although it will generally tolerate any reasonably good soil. Glossy abelia makes an excellent garden space divider or foundation planting.

Abutilon spp.

Flowering maple, Chinese lantern

BLOOM TIME: spring–autumn

HEIGHT/WIDTH: 8' × 8' (2.5 × 2.5m)

LIGHT: full sun

ZONES: 9–10

OTHER: possible indoor plant

Flowering maple

The eye-catching dangling bell- or cup-shaped flowers quite resemble Chinese lanterns (hence one of the shrub's common names), and in some areas may bloom almost continuously. Just looking at a photograph will make you want at least one of the hundred and fifty *Abutilon* species. The cultivar 'Canary Bird' has lemon yellow flowers that grow to almost 3 inches (8cm) long. 'Kentish Belle' boasts flowers with apricot-yellow petals, red calyxes, and purple stamens. There are also reds, whites, oranges, and a plethora of purples, from the palest lilac to a dark, saucer-flowered cultivar called 'Violetta'.

While this plant grows as a garden shrub only in very warm regions, hybrid flowering maple is often used as a border plant in cooler areas, where it will grow only 12 to 18 inches (30 to 45cm) tall. It can be moved indoors for the winter, as it is not hardy enough to survive outdoors.

Give this rapidly growing, somewhat rangy shrub a wind-free, well-drained, warm growing site with moist soil. Flowering maple is also a decorative patio shrub when grown in a container, and is easily pruned to size.

Aesculus parviflora

Bottlebrush buckeye

BLOOM TIME: midsummer

HEIGHT/WIDTH: 12' × 12' (3.5 × 3.5m)

LIGHT: sun with afternoon shade–partial shade–full
shade

ZONES: 5–9

OTHER: attracts butterflies

Bottlebrush buckeye

If you have a problem growing anything substantial under a large shade tree, this wide-spreading, hardy, deciduous shrub may amply fill the space. Small white flowers with red anthers appear in 8- to 12-inch (20–30cm) -long, narrow, upright clusters showing well above dark green, coarse-textured foliage. Leaves turn yellow in autumn, providing late-season interest. Ovoid, smooth-skinned fruits containing one or more large blackish brown seeds (which are poisonous if eaten) follow the flowers; stems bearing the seeds are popular in flower arrangements.

The best soil for growing bottlebrush buckeye is moist, well-drained, and improved only with organic amendments. Although not truly invasive, this rangy shrub, also called "horse chestnut," does sucker. Prune suckers off and use them to propagate new shrubs. If you prefer a suckerless variety, be sure to purchase *Aesculus parviflora* 'Roger's', which has even longer white flower clusters.

Amelanchier laevis

Allegheny serviceberry, shadblow

BLOOM TIME: spring

HEIGHT/WIDTH: 25' × 18' (7.5 × 5.5m)

LIGHT: partial sun

ZONES: 5–9

OTHER: attracts birds, honeybees

Allegheny serviceberry

Covered with profuse clusters of white flowers in early spring when, theoretically, the shad are running, this graceful shrub is native to coastal areas and wetlands of eastern North America. Black, sweet, summer berries were prized by Native Americans long before colonists arrived to share the crops. Birds are also fans of the fruit, so the berries rarely stay around for long. Dark green leaves turn a lovely orange in autumn.

Deciduous serviceberry thrives best in moist, acidic, organic soils with good drainage. No pruning is necessary, except for occasional suckers. Because of its upright growth with spreading branches, this shrub can also be trained as a small tree. Watch out for fireblight, borers, various mites, and powdery mildew.

Plant Allegheny serviceberry by a pond, in a seaside garden, or at the edge of a woodland. They especially complement other native shrubs. There are many other worthy *Amelanchier* species, including *A. alnifolia* and *A. grandiflora*.

Aronia arbutifolia

Red chokeberry

BLOOM TIME: spring

HEIGHT/WIDTH: $7' \times 7'$ $(2 \times 2m)$

LIGHT: full sun–partial shade

ZONES: 5–9

OTHER: attracts birds

Red chokeberry

Bright red, pea-size berries appear in late summer and persevere through winter, a hallmark of this deciduous shrub. Berries are framed by 3-inch (7cm) leaves that turn from dark green to bright reddish purple in early autumn if the shrub receives enough sun. Small white flowers that resemble apple blossoms appear in late spring. For prime flowering and fruiting, give this tolerant plant full sun, although it does nicely in partial shade.

This versatile shrub thrives in moist soil, though it will tolerate soil that is slightly dry. Chokeberry's suckering habit dictates that it is best placed at the back of a border rather than used as a specimen shrub. But the suckers make it easy to propagate the plant, since they root readily if taken in springtime. There is also a black chokeberry, *A. melanocarpa*, which is somewhat shorter and bears shiny black fruits in autumn.

Berberis spp.

Barberry

BLOOM TIME: early spring

HEIGHT/WIDTH: 3'–8' × 3'–8' (1–2.4m × 1–2.4m)

LIGHT: full sun–partial shade

ZONES: 4–7, depending on species

OTHER: attracts birds, honeybees; good cut flower

'Boughton's Gold' barberry

There are many barberries, both deciduous and evergreen, to choose from, and all are useful, easy-to-grow garden shrubs. Small, handsome leaves cover thorny branches, which make barberry a formidable barrier hedge. Many species display autumn foliage color, and in spring pretty yellow flowers accent barberry. These blooms are followed by oval red or purple berries.

Barberries perform quite well in average soil and need minimal watering. They are generally pest- and disease-free, though some species, particularly *B. vulgaris*, are hosts to black stem rust, which can be transmitted to wheat. Some wheat-growing states have banned the planting of certain barberry species, so be sure to check with your local agricultural extension office before installing any new barberries.

Popular barberries include the deciduous Japanese barberry (*B. thunbergii*), a widely adaptable upright-growing shrub that is hardy to Zone 5; wintergreen barberry (*B. julianae*), a hardy (to Zone 5) evergreen shrub; and Korean barberry (*B. koreana*), a deciduous shrub that can be grown as far north as Zone 4.

Bruckenthalia spiculifolia

Spike heath

BLOOM TIME: late spring–early summer

HEIGHT/WIDTH: 8" × 12" (20 × 30cm)

LIGHT: full sun

ZONES: 6–8

Spike heath

If you need a shrub groundcover and like the appearance of heather, consider spike heath. Low-growing and somewhat sprawling, its ½-inch (1cm) -long, needlelike, dark green leaves densely cover shoots and persist all year long. In late spring or early summer, very small, clustered, rosy pink bell-shaped flowers seem to almost cover the plant in long racemes. Another bonus is that the flowers are sweetly fragrant. And even past their prime, the flower heads are quite attractive, though deadheading faded flowers will result in lusher foliage.

Like heathers, heaths prefer moist, lime-free, peaty soil in full sun. Spike heath is an excellent choice for rocky ground; its roots penetrate deeply, and once the plant is established it is tolerant of drought. In cold-winter regions, the shrubs will benefit from a cover of pine boughs. Some aficionados create a special mixed species garden just for heaths and heathers.

Brunfelsia pauciflora
(B. calycina)

Yesterday, today, and tomorrow

BLOOM TIME: spring–early summer

HEIGHT/WIDTH: 3' × 3' (1 × 1m)

LIGHT: partial shade

ZONES: 7–10

Yesterday, today, and tomorrow

You'll have to fuss a bit with yesterday, today, and tomorrow in order to enjoy the clustered, pansylike, 2-inch (5cm) -wide flowers. The blooms are also pleasantly fragrant. This shrub takes its rather unwieldy name from its changing appearance: flowers appear on the first day as white-centered, intensely dark purple blooms then pale to lavender and finally change to white within two days. While the most active flowering takes place in spring and early summer, this unusual shrub may flower almost constantly in frost-free regions.

Rich, lime-free, well-drained soil is just one of this shrub's many requirements. Determined watering and regular fertilization are also mandatory. Occasionally pinching off the ends of stems will keep the shrub attractively bushy. Some gardeners grow yesterday, today, and tomorrow in a greenhouse in order to best meet all its needs, but others place this evergreen in containers on a sheltered patio or near an entranceway, where they will be constantly reminded to offer tender loving care. Yesterday, today, and tomorrow can also be grown as a flowering houseplant.

Buddleia alternifolia

Fountain butterfly bush

BLOOM TIME: early summer

HEIGHT/WIDTH: 12' × 12' (3.5 × 3.5m)

LIGHT: full sun

ZONES: 5–9

OTHER: attracts butterflies; good cut flower

Fountain butterfly bush

In spring, butterflies decorate the lightly fragrant lilac waterfall that nearly blankets the small, fine-textured, forest green leaves of fountain butterfly bush. The gracefully arching branches of deciduous *Buddleia alternifolia* also make it an excellent small willowlike tree if trained to shape.

Initially discovered in China in 1875, the *Buddleia* genus was named after the Reverend Adam Buddle, a noted amateur English botanist. New *Buddleia* shrub varieties appear all the time, all carrying the signature trait of attracting butterflies.

A related species, *B. davidii*, blooms throughout the summer, and allows you to select for color as well as scent.

'Royal Red', 'Pink Pearl', 'Empire Blue', 'Burgundy', and 'Black Knight' are among the multiple selections, which grow from 10 to 15 feet (3 to 4.5m) tall.

All butterfly bushes are easy to grow, thriving in most well-drained soils if given sufficient sun and regular watering. They even do well near the sea, and tolerate pollution. The bush will often die to the ground with the winter, but will generally return in spring; *B. alternifolia* is the hardiest butterfly bush but may lose a season of bloom due to heavy winterkill.

Caesalpnia pulcherrima
(Poinciana pulcherrima)

Pride of Barbados

BLOOM TIME: late spring to early autumn

HEIGHT/WIDTH: 10' × 10' (3 × 3m)

LIGHT: full sun

ZONES: 9–11

OTHER: attracts hummingbirds

Pride of Barbados

Pride of Barbados is the island of Barbados' national flower. Each fiery red or yellow five-petaled flower has ten conspicuously long red stamens. Flowers, which are 1½ inches (3.5 cm) wide, are grouped on 12-inch (30cm) -long erect racemes. The attractive leaves are fernlike and dark green. Note that the pods, which contain seeds, can cause serious illness if ingested.

If your growing area suffers a cold spell, this semitropical plant may freeze to the ground, but it very well may come back quickly in spring. Pride of Barbados is also amenable to heavy pruning, if you want to control the shrub's size and shape. Grow this fine screening shrub in hot sun, in good, well-drained soil. Infrequent, deep watering is usually sufficient.

Callistemon citrinus

Lemon bottlebrush

BLOOM TIME: summer (spring–autumn in warm
climates)

HEIGHT/WIDTH: 15' × 7' (4.5 × 2m)

LIGHT: full sun

ZONES: 9–11

Lemon bottlebrush

Although most often called lemon bottlebrush, the less commonly used name crimson bottlebrush better suits this evergreen shrub, since its flowers are bright scarlet. Blooms, which are large and fuzzy, are clustered in profuse 4-inch (10cm) groups. The leaves, when crushed, emit a lemony scent, hence the species name "citrinus." Foliage starts off a reddish color but turns to green as the leaves mature.

Scarlet flowers are also the hallmark of the related species *Callistemon linearis*, but if you want yellow flower groups, look for *C. pallidus*, which is often recommended as a windbreak. The vigorous *C. salignus* has creamy yellow flowers.

Bottlebrushes are Australian natives, which means that they love strong sun, but adjust to cold spells with a sturdy mien. Poor soils, even those with some lime or salt, don't traumatize bottlebrush, and they thrive in semidry surroundings once they become established.

Hummingbirds fixate on the flowers, and small birds use the shrub as shelter. Lemon bottlebrush can be easily pruned to tree shape as it matures; simply prune side branches so that a single trunk remains.

Calluna vulgaris

Scotch heather

BLOOM TIME: midsummer to late autumn

HEIGHT/WIDTH: 4'–24' (10–60cm)

LIGHT: full sun

ZONES: 4–7

OTHER: attracts honeybees; flowers good for cutting
and drying

Mixed cultivars of Scotch heather

This is the moorland plant of Europe, where lime-free, moist, peaty soil is the natural growing medium. In other regions you will have to re-create these conditions, but if you can do so successfully, heathers will grow quite vigorously.

Small, bell-shaped flowers grouped on spikes are long-lasting. Some cultivars are excellent for drying too, such as the double white 'Alba Plena', the double silvery pink 'Elsie Purnell', and the deep pink 'Peter Sparkes'. Overlapping, scale-like leaves provide a gray-green backdrop for the bright flowers. Leaves develop a purple tinge in winter.

Heathers, as a group, are low-growing plants, ranging in height from 4 inches (10cm) to about 3 feet (90cm), depending on the variety. You may consider the smaller heathers for groundcover use as well as for edging sub-shrubs. All heathers make excellent additions to a rock garden. Heathers and heaths (*Erica* spp.) are often grown together, and many aficionados create special gardens for these lovely plants.

Calycanthus floridus

Sweetshrub

BLOOM TIME: spring–summer

HEIGHT/WIDTH: 8' × 8' (2.5 × 2.5m)

LIGHT: light shade–partial shade–full shade

ZONES: 5–9

OTHER: good cut branches

'Athens' sweetshrub

Strawberry-scented, burgundy-red, 2-inch (5cm) -wide flowers that appear in midsummer are the chief attraction of this hardy deciduous shrub. The flowers are most fragrant on warm days, and were once commonly used as potpourri to freshen homes. Shiny, dark green, 5-inch (12cm) -long leaves turn yellow in autumn.

Native to eastern North America, and often found along stream banks, sweetshrub grows best in moist, well-drained, loam augmented by leaf mold or peat moss. Pruning is largely unnecessary except for removal of dead wood in spring and a bit of thinning if branches become crowded.

Plant this shrub near a porch, patio, or window so that you can best enjoy its unusual fragrance and to offer it some protection. Make note that its seeds, if ingested in large quantities, can cause illness, but the pods are only produced every couple of years.

Sweetshrub has several other common names, including "sweet-scented shrub," "strawberry shrub," "sweet bubby bush," and "Carolina allspice." For variety, try *C. floridus* 'Athens', which bears fragrant yellow flowers, or *C. floridus* 'Edith Wilder', which has wine-scented flowers.

Camellia japonica

Common camellia

BLOOM TIME: late winter–spring

HEIGHT/WIDTH: 7'–10' × 5'–7' (2–3 × 1.5–2m)

LIGHT: light shade

ZONES: 7–8

OTHER: good cut flower

'Admiral Nimitz' common camellia

If their growing conditions are well met, these lovely shrubs can be quite long-lived; one of the oldest camellias in the United States, planted in 1786, still grows in a specialty garden near Charleston, South Carolina. Once confined to the greenhouses of wealthy eighteenth-century plant collectors, camellias later became the darlings of Victorian gardeners and are now an integral part of modern horticulture.

The common camellia bears large, delicate flowers of white, pink, or red, and is covered in shiny dark green leaves.

This tender evergreen performs best when shaded from strong direct sunlight, and may be placed under the protec-

tion of tall trees. Note, though, that too much shade will inhibit flowering. Moist, well-drained, somewhat acidic organic soil and regular fertilizing are additional growing requirements of the common camellia. A deep mulch may also be helpful. If their needs are well met, camellias belie their delicate appearance.

Popular *Camellia japonica* cultivars available include 'Bob Hope', which bears dark red flowers; 'Elegans Supreme', which has salmon-pink flowers, and 'Lavinia Maggi', with double flowers striped red, pink, and white.

Carissa grandiflora

Natal plum

BLOOM TIME: all year

HEIGHT/WIDTH: 7' × 7' (2 × 2m)

LIGHT: full sun

ZONES: 9–11

Natal plum

Natal plum is unusual in that its white, star-shaped, 2-inch (5cm) -wide, fragrant flowers appear throughout the year. The flowers are followed by bright red, 2-inch (5cm) -long, plum-shaped fruit. While the fruit is edible, its seeds are poisonous. Because flowering occurs all year long, both flowers and ripe fruit often appear on the shrubs at the same time. Natal plum's attractive oval leaves are a shiny medium green.

The taller versions of this thorny evergreen South African native make a good screen when pruned lightly and a barrier hedge when pruned heavily. Shorter cultivars, such as *C. grandiflora* 'Tuttlei' do well in containers. Spreading dwarf cultivars 'Nana' and 'Boxwood Beauty' will grow to a height of only 18 inches (45cm) if they are pruned regularly.

Natal plums should not be placed near walkways because of the thorns. This semihardy shrub requires only ordinary well-drained garden soil and regular watering, but is susceptible to spider mites. Seaside conditions are tolerated.

Caryopteris × clandonensis

Blue spirea

BLOOM TIME: late summer–early autumn

HEIGHT/WIDTH: 2' × 2' (.6 × .6m)

LIGHT: full sun–light shade

ZONES: 6–9

OTHER: attracts butterflies, honeybees

'Longwood Blue' blue spirea

It isn't always easy to bring shades of blue into the garden, but this low-growing deciduous shrub accomplishes this goal quite effectively with the small-clustered flowers of cultivars such as 'Azure', 'Blue Mist', 'Kew Blue', 'Longwood Blue', 'Arthur Simmonds', and 'Heavenly Blue', among others. The foliage, which has a spicy aroma when crushed, is usually silvery green, although 'Worcester Gold' has bright yellow to chartreuse leaves.

Moderately hardy, blue spirea, nicknamed "bluebeard" in some growing areas, will sometimes die to the ground in colder regions, but most likely will resurrect itself in the spring. Hard pruning stimulates fresh growth and a pleasing shape.

Blue spirea is a good border plant in very well-drained garden sites; it seems to thrive in dry surroundings. Cutting back growth after each wave of blooms results in even more flowers. Complement the vibrant blue of this handsome shrub with yellow tones in other shrubs or perennials planted nearby.

Ceanothus americanus

New Jersey tea

BLOOM TIME: midsummer

HEIGHT/WIDTH: 3' × 3' (1 × 1m)

LIGHT: full sun

ZONES: 4–8

OTHER: attracts honeybees

New Jersey tea

The dense white flower clusters of New Jersey tea display themselves at the tips of the branches in high summer. Glossy dark green leaves grow up to 2 inches (5cm) long; in autumn interesting reddish fruits appear.

Intriguing as a single specimen within a bed of perennials or when planted in groups of varying sizes, New Jersey tea performs best in garden conditions similar to those of the Eastern forests where it grows wild. Give New Jersey tea a warm, dry site with light, humus-rich soil containing lime. Waterlogged soil is not tolerated. The shrub may die to the ground in winter, but will usually grow back full force in the spring. The blooms are carried on new wood, so dieback does not affect flowering.

Many gardeners use this hardy deciduous shrub for banks and semi-wild areas, since it adapts readily to poor growing conditions and needs no care. New Jersey tea has many regional names, including redroot, mountain sweet, and wild snowball.

Chaenomeles japonica

Japanese flowering quince

BLOOM TIME: spring

HEIGHT/WIDTH: 4' × 8' (1.2 × 2.5m)

LIGHT: full sun

ZONES: 5–9

OTHER: attracts birds

'Texas Scarlet' Japanese flowering quince

Japanese flowering quince, an undemanding woody plant, is equally at home in suburban backyards or in expansive country gardens. Low-growing varieties, such as reddish orange–flowering 'Orange Delight', are sometimes used as groundcover, to add dimension to a rock garden, or to balance a background of taller woody plants. Taller varieties, such as red flowering 'Minerva', find use as individual specimens, in grouped shrub plantings, or as thorny hedges.

The blooms of Japanese flowering quince are surrounded by 2-inch (5cm) -long shiny green leaves.

Yellowish fruits, which are many-seeded, round, sweet-smelling and 1 -inch (2.5cm) long, follow the flowers. Unless eaten by birds, the fruits may remain on the shrub through the middle of winter, extending seasonal interest.

Tolerant of pollution and city sites, these sturdy shrubs need only ordinary well-drained garden soil and regular watering. If you like bonsai, consider growing the delicate cultivar 'Pygmaea', which bears beautiful double apricot-pink flowers.

Clethra alnifolia

Summersweet

BLOOM TIME: midsummer

HEIGHT/WIDTH: $7' \times 7'$ (2×2m)

LIGHT: full sun–partial shade

ZONES: 3–9

OTHER: attracts honeybees

Summersweet

Native to swamps and woodlands, this slow-growing deciduous shrub naturally prefers moist, or even wet, growing conditions. While this shrub (which is sometimes listed as *Clethra paniculata* in catalogs) is not easy to establish, the long-lasting, exquisite spicy scent of its pink to white, 4-inch (10cm) -long flower clusters make summersweet worth a little extra effort. The dark green shiny leaves are attractive even when the shrub is not in bloom; expect the foliage to turn golden yellow in autumn.

Plant summersweet in early spring, give it quite ample water the first year, and make sure to mulch heavily to improve your odds of success.

There's a useful compact cultivar of summersweet called 'Hummingbird'; another good one is known as 'Ruby Spice', which boasts dark pink flowers, adapts well to salty winds and seacoast life. Summersweet was nicknamed "Sailor's Delight" by those who enjoyed its fragrance wafting on the breeze as ships pulled out to sea.

Cornus mas

Cornelian cherry

BLOOM TIME: late winter

HEIGHT/WIDTH: 15' × 10' (3 × 3m)

LIGHT: full sun

ZONES: 5–8

OTHER: attracts birds; good cut flowering branches

Cornelian cherry

Cornelian cherry, a welcome harbinger of spring, is one of the earliest of the flowering shrubs, and boasts masses of petite yellow blossoms that decorate bare branches in late winter. Leaves are shiny, green, 3-inch (7cm) ovals that turn yellow in autumn, with the cultivar 'Elegantissima' sporting gold-edged leaves flushed with pink. This fine cultivar is harder to find but worth looking for. Carmine-red, barrel shaped, 1-inch (2.5cm) fruits provide startling autumn color, and become edible after first frost—that is, if the birds permit leftovers.

'Golden Glory' is a more columnar version of cornelian cherry, and grows to 20 feet (6m) tall. 'Rosea', a pink-flowered cultivar, blooms a bit later than the species.

This warmth-loving shrub needs regular watering, but it's just about pest-free. Cornelian cherry can also be pruned into a small, spreading, and rather open specimen tree. In winter, gray and tan flaking bark helps provide year-round interest.

Cotinus coggygria

Smoke bush

BLOOM TIME: spring

HEIGHT/WIDTH: 10' × 10' (3 × 3m)

LIGHT: full sun

ZONES: 5–8

OTHER: good branches for arrangements

'Royal Purple' smoke bush

Royal purple foliage gives a stunning look all summer to many varieties of this large multistemmed shrub. Native to southern Europe and central China, smoke bush has long been a favorite of gardeners and remains exceedingly popular today. The yellow flowers aren't particularly noticeable, the common name "smoke bush" being earned because of the multiple smoky pink, fuzzy, fading flower stalks that persist until early autumn, providing welcome garden interest. Note that only female plants produce the "smoke," so if you are interested in the smoky effect, be sure to purchase a female shrub.

Grow this regal plant in any well-drained garden soil, including poor or rocky ground. To avoid mildew, give smoke bush full sun. Water regularly when the shrub is young, then cut back older stems in spring to encourage vigorous new growth.

Commonly found purple-leafed varieties include the attractive and hardy 'Royal Purple', 'Velvet Cloak', and 'Purpureus'. Leaf color changes to a beautiful red-purple in autumn, an extra bonus.

Cotoneaster apiculatus

Cranberry cotoneaster

Cranberry cotoneaster

BLOOM TIME: midsummer

HEIGHT/WIDTH: $3' \times 8'$ (1×2.5m)

LIGHT: full sun

ZONES: 5–7

OTHER: attracts birds, honeybees; bonsai

Small, round, red fruit practically covers this low-growing, vigorous, cotoneaster in early autumn. Fruit persists for a long period if birds or chipmunks don't get to it first, though they probably will. The fruits are a bit larger than those of other cotoneasters, about the size of cranberries, which earned this species its common name.

Framing the fruit are small, dark green, glossy leaves that turn reddish purple in late autumn. The following summer, petite red-tinged flowers appear. Cranberry cotoneaster has a spreading habit, and when the growing branches reach a flat surface such as the ground or a wall they will spread along it in an attractive fan shape.

Give this deciduous shrub average, well-drained soil that is slightly on the dry side. This is a low-maintenance shrub once it gets started, however, you must plant it where it is to grow as it doesn't transplant well. If you have very limited garden space but want bright green leaves, red autumn color, and red berries, consider the dwarf cultivar 'Tom Thumb' for container use.

Cotoneaster divaricatus

Spreading cotoneaster

BLOOM TIME: midsummer

HEIGHT/WIDTH: 6' × 6' (1.8 × 1.8m)

LIGHT: full sun

ZONES: 5–7

OTHER: attracts birds, honeybees

Spreading cotoneaster

Profuse rose-tinged white flowers, each ½-inch (12mm) wide, bloom in spring, but spreading cotoneaster's main attraction is its small, conspicuous, ⅜-inch (10mm) coral red berries, which appear in autumn. This wide-spreading, medium-height deciduous shrub grows wild in central and western China. Dark green shiny leaves on arching branches turn scarlet-red in autumn.

Like most cotoneasters, this species does well in average, well-drained soil that is allowed to become somewhat dry between regular waterings. If given a good start, spreading cotoneaster will thrive in poor soil too. While some gardeners like this as an individual plant across from a view window so they can watch birds enjoy the berries, the prime use of spreading cotoneaster is as a picturesque informal hedge.

Cytisus × praecox

Warminster broom

BLOOM TIME: spring

HEIGHT/WIDTH: 6' × 6' (1.8 × 1.8m)

LIGHT: full sun

ZONES: 6–9

'Moonlight' Warminster broom

In springtime, the arching branchlets of Warminster broom are completely covered with ½-inch (1cm) -wide, creamy yellow flowers that resemble those of pea plants, to which they are related. The scent is considered by many to be unpleasant, so you may wish to plant Warminster broom away from the house.

Hairy 1-inch (2.5cm) seedpods, which may cause mild stomach upset if ingested, follow bloom. Small medium green leaves tend to drop early. To keep this semihardy Mediterranean native content, give it dryish, mostly lime-free, well-drained soil in sun.

Plant warmth-loving Warminster broom in the company of compatible heathers, heaths, junipers, and birches, where it makes an excellent specimen shrub. Warminster broom also performs well as a hedge.

The cultivar 'Allgold' has cascades of soft golden yellow flowers, while the bicolored 'Hollandia' has pale pink to cerise flower centers, with the rest of the petals in the same shade as the species. 'Gold Spear', which reaches only 3 feet (90cm) in height, displays golden flowers; 'Moonlight' has flowers in a pale silvery yellow.

Daboecia cantabrica

(also D. polifolia)

Irish heath

BLOOM TIME: late spring–early summer

HEIGHT/WIDTH: 2' × 2' (.6 × .6m)

LIGHT: full sun

ZONES: 6–8

Irish heath

Delicate, pink, white, or purple bell-shaped flowers held in racemes 3 to 6 inches (7 to 15cm) long dangle from the branches of this charming dwarf evergreen shrub. Irish heath is not actually a heath (*Erica* spp.) or a heather (*Calluna* spp.), but rather a low-growing shrub that resembles heaths.

This semihardy plant is sure to thrive if you are able to create its preferred conditions, which include regular watering, excellent drainage, and acidic soil mixed with an equal amount of peat moss. Use a permanent protective mulch of ground bark or chunky peat moss. Nourish Irish heath in spring with a light application of azalea fertilizer.

Irish heath is a good choice for a rock garden, where it will receive the sharp drainage it requires. Or you may wish to plant it among azaleas and rhododendrons (*Rododendron* spp.), which share a need for the same growing conditions.

If you can meet the cultural requirements of Irish heath, consider several excellent cultivars, including 'W. Buchanan' and 'Atropurpurea', both with rose-purple flowers, or 'Alba' and 'David Moss', which bear white flowers. 'David Moss' is especially good for cut flowers, either arranged fresh or dried.

Daphne × burkwoodii

Burkwood daphne

BLOOM TIME: spring–early summer

HEIGHT/WIDTH: 3'–4' × 4'–5' (1–1.2 × 1.2–1.5m)

LIGHT: full sun–partial shade

ZONES: 5–8

'Carol Mackie' Burkwood daphne

Daphnes in general are inclined to be temperamental, but if you simply must have that delectable fragrance in your garden, Burkwood daphne is among the easiest of the forty species to grow. Pale pink flowers grow in 2-inch (5cm) -wide clusters among narrow, pale green leaves. Foliage may be variegated on some cultivars, including the popular 'Carol Mackie'. Small, reddish fruits follow the flowers.

Burkwood daphne requires a well-drained, neutral soil, and is improved by mulching. It does best in full sun, but will tolerate some shade during the day. Water the shrubs sparingly, as they don't adapt well to wet soils. Feed Burkwood daphne each spring with a fertilizer appropriate for rhododendrons.

Fruits, flowers, leaves, and bark are highly toxic if ingested, and contact with sap may irritate skin. Since daphnes resent transplanting, make sure to place them where they will remain permanently. Note that Burkwood daphne is also an excellent daphne for containers, where its scent can be appreciated from nearby sitting areas.

Daphne odora

Winter daphne

BLOOM TIME: early spring

HEIGHT/WIDTH: 6' × 6' (1.8 × 1.8m)

LIGHT: partial shade

ZONES: 7–9

OTHER: attracts birds

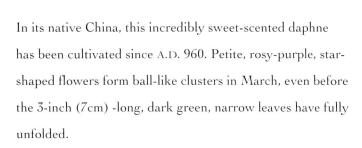

'Marginata' winter daphne

In its native China, this incredibly sweet-scented daphne has been cultivated since A.D. 960. Petite, rosy-purple, star-shaped flowers form ball-like clusters in March, even before the 3-inch (7cm) -long, dark green, narrow leaves have fully unfolded.

Purchase daphne in containers, and plant it in early spring or autumn in the spot it is to remain, as moving this evergreen seldom succeeds. Slow to get started, and a some-times a finicky grower, winter daphne may reach a rounded 6 feet (1.8m) in height and width. Its natural globe shape

may be helped along by judicious pruning. Best adapted to partial shade, winter daphne requires very well-drained soil rich in organic matter, and does best with a leaf mulch.

All parts of the plant are poisonous, especially the berries, so it is probably best to avoid planting this shrub if children are often about. Otherwise, place winter daphne where you can enjoy its strikingly delicious fragrance. The cultivar 'Marginata' offers distinctive leaves with cream-colored margins.

Deutzia gracilis

Slender deutzia

BLOOM TIME: spring

HEIGHT/WIDTH: 4'–6' × 4'–6' (1.2–1.8 × 1.2–1.8m)

LIGHT: full sun–light shade

ZONES: 5–8

OTHER: good branches for cutting

Slender deutzia

Named after J.D. van der Deutz, a Dutch alderman and supporter of horticultural adventures, this very old garden favorite is amazingly easy to grow: any reasonably good garden soil is fine as long as the shrub receives regular watering.

Glorious clusters of pure white, fragrant flowers on slender stems cover this mounding deutzia like snow in springtime for as long as two weeks. While the blooms are spectacular and prolific, they are scentless, which is actually a plus for some gardeners but a big minus for others. Attractive, bright green, 2-inch (5cm) -long leaves appear after the flowers. For an additional eye-catcher, look for the cultivar 'Variegata', which has green and yellow variegated leaves.

Since this shrub tends toward the inconspicuous after spring bombastics, place slender deutzia among other shrubs where it will peacefully blend in. Occasionally, depending on weather, winter dieback does occur. Prune the dead wood out in spring for the best plant appearance. While slender deutzia prefers full sun, it will happily tolerate light shade.

Elaeagnus pungens

Thorny eleagnus, silverberry

BLOOM TIME: autumn

HEIGHT/WIDTH: 10' × 10' (3 × 3m)

LIGHT: full sun–partial shade

ZONES: 7–9

'Fruitlandii' thorny eleagnus

For a thorny boundary hedge or an impenetrable screen, consider thorny eleagnus, which offers small, silvery, gardenia-scented flowers as an additional bonus. The blooms appear in autumn, somewhat unusual in itself, and are followed by red fruits in spring. Leaves are about 4 inches (10cm) long, and are gray-green with rust-colored dots, so the shrub blends easily into the overall landscape.

This fast-growing evergreen thrives in just about any garden soil, including that oceanfront yard corner that seems to mean certain death for other plants. Wind doesn't bother thorny eleagnus; nor does heat or intermittent drought.

It's best to prune this shrub heavily in midsummer for size control and to encourage dense foliage, particularly if used as a hedge windbreak. Thorny eleagnus may be either sheared for use as a formal hedge or clipped with garden shears for a more natural shape.

The cultivar 'Maculata' has green leaves with a gold mark in the center, while 'Variegata' offers leaves with cream-colored edges.

Erica carnea
(E. herbacea)

Spring heath

BLOOM TIME: midwinter–early spring

HEIGHT/WIDTH: 6'–12' × 16"–24" (15–30 × 40–60cm)

LIGHT: full sun (except in very hot areas)

ZONES: 5–7

OTHER: attracts butterflies; good cut flowers

Spring heath

Related to heathers (*Calluna* spp.), heaths require similar cultural conditions. If you have heavy clay soil, you will need to do quite a bit of improvement before you put in any heath, as lime kills special root bacteria that help transfer nutrients from the soil to the plant. Although spring heath is more tolerant than most other species, to forestall starvation provide a bedding of peat moss, compost, and sand, accompanied by superb drainage. Regular watering is necessary.

Planted in the soil they prefer, cared for well, and mulched regularly, these compact evergreen shrubs will reward you handsomely with rosy red, purple, rich pink, or white bell-shaped flowers. The blooms appear in profusion amidst needlelike, dense, pale or dark green foliage. While most spring heaths bloom in late winter and spring, the aptly named cultivar 'Winter Beauty' may be more suitable as a Christmas present.

Most heaths are sure butterfly beckoners. Plant spring heath in groups of five or more for a taller, shrubby groundcover. Cutting spent flowers will help keep the shrub in good shape.

Euonymus alatus

Winged euonymus, burning bush

BLOOM TIME: late spring–summer

HEIGHT/WIDTH: 8' × 10' (2.5 × 3m)

LIGHT: full sun–partial shade

ZONES: 4–9

'Compacta' winged euonymus

Almost unrivaled for its spectacular crimson red autumn leaf color, this ultra-hardy deciduous shrub needs ample space in the garden. While winged euonymus does bear flowers, they are rather insignificant, and the shrub's other virtues are the main reasons for growing it. Use several winged euonymus as a background hedge, and admire the seasonal changes: blue-green, 3-inch (7cm) -long leaves and small yellowish flowers in summer; reddish purple, pea-sized fruit and brilliant, long-term color in autumn; and branches that usually exhibit prominent corky wings in winter. If you want to be certain to have these corky wings for use in floral arrangements, seek out the cultivar 'Monstrosus'.

Spreading by nature, slow-growing winged euonymus is easily trimmed to satisfaction. Adaptable to all but wet soils, there are no serious pest or disease annoyances. Happy in sun or partial shade, the main difference between the two situations is some color variation in the leaves. 'Compacta' is a dwarf cultivar, as is the new 'Rudy Haag', which is even smaller. Both are just as autumn-bright, though they lack the corky "wings" on the branches.

Exochorda × macrantha

Pearlbush

BLOOM TIME: spring

HEIGHT/WIDTH: 4' × 7' (1.2 × 2m)

LIGHT: full sun

ZONES: 5–9

OTHER: attracts butterflies

'The Bride' pearlbush

The strings of pearly buds on this small, white-flowering shrub have lent it the common name "pearlbush." If you are a somewhat intermittent gardener, pearlbush might suit, since it tolerates some neglect. Well-drained soil, not overly alkaline, regular water, and full sun are its only requests.

Plant pearlbush in a mixed border with brightly colored perennials and annuals, as this shrub can be rather demure except when displaying its multitude of 1-inch (2.5cm) flowers.

Pearlbush has no objection to having its medium green foliage pruned for shape, and in fact, a good pruning will help the shrub maintain its shape. Cut out weak branches after the pretty flowers have faded to promote a fuller shape, as pearlbush has a tendency to get somewhat leggy, especially when it is young.

Pearlbush is best planted in spring, as a container-grown or balled and burlapped species, since bareroot plants have a tougher time getting established.

If you have a small garden space and require a more compact shrub, look for the cultivar 'The Bride', which grows only 3 feet (1m) tall and as wide.

Feijoa sellowiana

Pineapple guava

BLOOM TIME: spring

HEIGHT/WIDTH: 15' × 15' (4.5 × 4.5m)

LIGHT: full sun

ZONES: 8–10

Pineapple guava

If you want a fruit tree in the South, and nothing else will tolerate that hot, sunny garden spot, pineapple guava just might do the trick. It is the hardiest of the subtropical fruits, and grows as a large multistemmed shrub unless pruned.

In springtime, white, thick-petaled, 1-inch (2.5cm) -wide flowers with startling crimson stamen tufts attract both birds and bees. Oval leaves, about 3 inches (7cm) long, are glossy green with silvery backing. If you have another plant to cross-pollinate, about five to seven months after bloom (as long as the shrub is given regular watering) you'll have ripe 2-inch-long, oval, gray-green fruit with whitish pineapple-flavored pulp. The fruit is good eaten fresh, and delicious in jellies and preserves.

Pineapple guava may also be pruned in late spring to create a small tree, hedge, or espalier. Pruning will also keep it to a manageable size, if you are gardening in a small space.

Varieties such as 'Coolidge', 'Beechwood', and 'Nazemete', are self-fertile, however cross-pollination improves the fruit crop.

Forsythia × intermedia

Golden bell, border forsythia

BLOOM TIME: early spring

HEIGHT/WIDTH: varies

LIGHT: full sun

ZONES: 6–9

OTHER: good for forcing indoors

Golden bell

In Southern regions, forsythias bloom as early as February, and have become a golden harbinger of springtime. Even in more northerly areas, forsythia is among the earliest flowering shrubs. To enjoy even earlier flowers, bring budded branches indoors and place them on a sunny windowsill in a vase of lukewarm water, where they will burst into glorious bloom.

There are many cultivars of border forsythia available, all hardy and all with profuse lemon yellow to bright gold flowers. Choose for size among the cultivars 'Fiesta' at 3 feet (1m) high, 'Minigold' at 5 feet (1.5m) high, or 'Variegeta' which grows to 6 feet (1.8m) and has foliage splashed with white.

Forsythia, named after English horticulturist William Forsythe, does well in a wide range of soils, but must have regular watering. Forsythia does well in full sun or partial shade; while it will grow in deep shade it will not flower to any significant degree. It is surprisingly effective against an evergreen background. Prune after flowering, following the natural habit of the shrub and removing old or dead wood.

Fothergilla major

Large fothergilla

BLOOM TIME: spring

HEIGHT/WIDTH: 6'–10' × 7' (1.8–3 × 2m)

LIGHT: full sun–partial shade

ZONES: 5–8

Large fothergilla

A favorite among gardeners who plant for autumn color, large fothergilla has leaves that turn yellow, then orange, and finally purple-red. Note, though, that autumn color may be inhibited if the shrub is grown in too much shade. Native to the rich moist woods of southeastern North America, this medium-sized deciduous shrub also bears small white, honey-scented, brushlike flowers in spring.

Pest-free, large fothergilla prefers moist, well-drained, acidic soil, but is adaptable to varying soil types as long as they are not alkaline. Plant this attractive shrub in spring or autumn, preferably on a sunny site. Where summers get quite hot, though, partial shade is best. Because large fothergilla is slow-growing, it will need only occasional pruning, which should be done after flowering.

A favorite specimen plant, large fothergilla is also eye-catching in groups. There are also dwarf fothergillas available, including *Fothergilla gardenii* 'Mt. Airy', which, like its bigger cousin, provides reliable, brilliant autumn color.

Gardenia augusta
(G. jasminoides)

Common gardenia

BLOOM TIME: late spring–autumn

HEIGHT/WIDTH: 2'–8' × 2'–8' (.6–2.5m × .6–2.5m)

LIGHT: full sun (light shade in hot climates)

ZONES: vary by cultivar

OTHER: very fragrant cut flower

Common gardenia

Sentimentalists who have fond memories of their fragrant white prom corsages will want to plant an evergreen gardenia near an entryway or potted up on a patio. Large, lush flowers with white waxy petals bloom among shiny dark green leaves.

Native to China and Japan, gardenia is available in many beautiful cultivars. 'White Gem' is the classic container gardenia, and grows only 2 feet (60cm) tall. For narrow entryways try 'Veitchii' or 'Kimura Shikazaki', which reach only 4 feet (1.2m) in height. There is also a plethora of taller hedge gardenias, the size of which can be easily controlled by pruning.

While most gardenias are hardy only in zones 8 to 10, 'Klein's Hardy' was specifically created for cold-winter climates and is supposed to withstand temperatures down to 0°F(17.78°C). Full sun is best in all but very hot climates, but light shade is tolerated.

Gardenias require very well-drained soil high in organic matter, and regular fertilizing with acid plant food or fish emulsion. Cut faded flowers to encourage new blooms and prune the shrub to promote a bushier habit. Plants may be visited by pesky whiteflies and aphids, but a strong water stream usually takes care of minor infestations.

Hamamelis mollis

Chinese witch hazel

BLOOM TIME: late winter–early spring

HEIGHT/WIDTH: 8' × 8' (2.5 × 2.5m)

LIGHT: full sun–light shade

ZONES: 5–9

OTHER: good cut branches

Chinese witch hazel

Almost unrivaled for dependable winter or early spring flowering, Chinese witch hazel bears 1½-inch (3.5cm) -wide, rich yellow, spidery flowers in February and March. The blooms, cradled in a red-brown base, bring summer glory far in advance of the season to bare stems. Better yet, the flowers are sweetly fragrant. In autumn, dark green woolly leaves change to a clear charming yellow.

For the best display, place this slow-growing, disease-resistant, deciduous shrub to highlight a dark backdrop.

With its tall and spreading, yet neat, habit, many gardeners like to use it as a specimen plant; it may also be grown as a small tree. Set witch hazel where it is to grow, since it dislikes transplanting. Slightly acid soil is best, with organic matter added. Witch hazels are popular shrubs for spacious city gardens, as they tolerate pollution and dry, gritty air. Water well until the shrub is established, but do not fertilize.

The cultivar 'Pallida' has sulfur yellow flowers and a slightly sweeter fragrance.

Hebe speciosa

Showy hebe

BLOOM TIME: late summer

HEIGHT/WIDTH: 2'–5' × 2'–5' (.6–1.5m × .6–1.5m)

LIGHT: full sun–partial shade

ZONES: 10–11

Showy hebe

Glossy evergreen leaves are a hallmark of this New Zealand native. In summer, deep reddish purple or bluish flowers are carried proudly on multiple dense 3-inch (7cm) -long racemes.

At its best in the seaside garden, showy hebe is also a city garden favorite, as it is tolerant of dust and pollution if watered regularly. Inland, in hot areas, showy hebe appreciates some light shade, but in a coastal location it fares quite well in full sun. Poor, light soil is its friend, which makes hebe very useful as an edging, groundcover, hedge, or shrub for the mixed border. But make certain drainage is good, as root rot can sneak into perpetually soggy soils.

For a change of pace, the cultivar 'Variegata' has leaves splashed with cream, while 'Imperialis' has magenta flowers accompanied by reddish leaves. Showy hebe also makes a nice, unfussy container plant for the patio.

Hibiscus syriacus

Rose of Sharon

BLOOM TIME: midsummer–autumn

HEIGHT/WIDTH: 6'–10' × 4' – 6' (1.8–3 × 1.2–1.8m)

LIGHT: full sun

ZONES: 5–9

OTHER: attracts butterflies, birds

Rose of Sharon

Native to China, this free-flowering deciduous shrub is quite hardy in warm gardens, and can be grown in colder areas against a reflecting wall. Exotic, trumpet-shaped flowers, 3 to 5 inches (7 to 12cm) in diameter, evoke reveries of tropical climes and a leisurely lifestyle. Whether the variety is pink, blue, or white, rose of Sharon provides color when many other flowers are finished for the season, although it does come into bloom later than most.

While the single-flowered varieties are the hardiest, nurseries often carry double-flowered types, such as 'Blushing Bride', which has bright pink blossoms, and 'Violaceus Plenus', which bears blue-purple blossoms.

Deep, well-drained, easily worked soil provides the best growing conditions. Make sure to move these plants only in spring, as they take some time to get established. A layer of mulch through the winter for the first few years will offer additional protection until rose of Sharon matures somewhat. Prune in spring to shape the shrub and fertilize monthly from April through August. Regular watering is a must.

Hippophae rhamnoides

Sea buckthorn

BLOOM TIME: spring

HEIGHT/WIDTH: 15' × 15' (4.5 × 4.5m)

LIGHT: full sun–light shade

ZONES: 3–8

Sea buckthorn

This common deciduous plant of seacoasts and river banks tolerates salty soils and actually prefers a sandy home, making it a gem for those living near waterfront sites. Suckers spread underground, preventing sandy dunes from shifting, so sea buckthorn is especially valuable for seaside gardeners. The shrub does, however, have long fierce spines on its branches, so set it back a distance from pathways.

Young shoots are glossy yellow-brown, and become dark brown with age. Small, dullish, yellow flowers appear before the leaves. However, the narrow, 2-inch (5cm) -long, silvery green leaves unfold from attractive golden brown leaf buds. Both male and female plants are needed to form the persistent and plentiful ½-inch (1cm) -wide, yellow-orange fruits, which appear in autumn. The berries are not appreciated by birds, so they stay on the shrubs, adding color to the winter landscape through the winter. For large-acreage screening, five females to one male plant works well with wind-blown pollination.

Hydrangea macrophylla

Big-leaved hydrangea

BLOOM TIME: summer

HEIGHT/WIDTH: 3'–6' × 3'–6' (1–1.8 × 1–1.8m)

LIGHT: full sun

ZONES: 6–9

'Nikko Blue' big-leaved hydrangea

In its native surroundings—Southern China, Japan, and the Himalayas—this deciduous hydrangea will grow to 10 feet (3m) in height. But in most gardens, about half that height is usual. Puffed "snowballs" of flowers appear in summer, when few other shrubs are in bloom.

Hydrangeas are especially fun for the chemically oriented, as the flowers may change color according to soil conditions. Pink-flowering varieties produce blue flowers when in acidic soils and red flowers when in alkaline soils. Because the soil's pH can be altered with fertilizer and additives, a pleasing array can be arranged in varying garden sections. Note, though, that white cultivars will not change flower color.

Moderately hardy, big-leaved hydrangea needs rich, moist soil and a sheltered site, and does best with a spring mulch. Many varieties are available, most of which give a clue as to their color: 'White Swan', 'Amethyst', 'Pink Monarch', 'Blue Wave', and so on. The cultivar 'Nikko Blue' is somewhat hardier in colder areas; it blooms on new wood, so that some winter dieback does not interfere with flowering.

Hydrangea paniculata 'Grandiflora'

PeeGee hydrangea

BLOOM TIME: summer–autumn

HEIGHT/WIDTH: 12' × 12' (3.5 × 3.5m)

LIGHT: full sun–partial shade

ZONES: 4–8

OTHER: dried flowers

PeeGee hydrangea

So common in rural North America that it almost seems a native, PeeGee hydrangea actually hails from Asia. A vigorous, late-blooming deciduous shrub, this hydrangea is often trained to tree form, that is, with a single trunk. Large, coarsely toothed leaves add impact to fluffy, white, pyramidal, flower clusters, each an immense 12 by 12 inches (30 by 30cm). The flowers, which start off a greenish white, turn first a purple-pink, then bronzy green with age. The exact flower color depends both on the pH, which should be slightly acid, and the soil's aluminum content.

PeeGee hydrangea makes a fine specimen shrub in a slightly sheltered position. You can remove lower branches to encourage a cascading form. Grow this lovely shrub in rich, moist soil. While it tolerates light shade, it prospers best in full sun. Mulch PeeGee hydrangea in winter, prune it in early spring, and fertilize after pruning. The dried flowers are stunning when gathered in easy winter bouquets (make sure to use garden gloves if you are possibly allergic to the foliage).

Hydrangea quercifolia

Oakleaf hydrangea

BLOOM TIME: spring–summer

HEIGHT/WIDTH: 3'–6' × 4'–6' (1–1.8 × 1.2–1.8m)

LIGHT: full sun–partial shade

ZONES: 5–9

OTHER: good cut flower

Oakleaf hydrangea

This rounded shrub has garden gifts for all seasons. As its botanical name indicates (*quercus* is the genus name of oak trees), the deeply lobed, 8-inch (20cm) leaves resemble those of oaks. The leaves, which are green in spring and summer, turn crimson, purple, or deep bronze in autumn. In winter, stems are a pleasing brown and exfoliate with age to display a darker, reddish brown interior.

When spring arrives, 10-inch (25cm) -long, pyramidal flower clusters appear. The flowers, fragrant and white, last for several weeks, turning pinkish purple as spring moves into summer.

This deciduous shrub is fast-growing and quite hardy when grown in a protected location in the northern reaches of its zone. It needs well-drained, richly organic, moist soil, regular watering, and some shade if you live in a truly hot area. In fact, this is the hydrangea species best suited to shade, so if you have your heart set on a hydrangea and have a shady yard, this is most likely your best bet. The cultivar 'Sikes Dwarf' makes a good shrub for a container.

Hypericum frondosum

Golden St. John's wort

BLOOM TIME: midsummer–autumn

HEIGHT/WIDTH: 3' × 3' (1 × 1m)

LIGHT: full sun–partial shade

ZONES: 6–8

'Sunburst' Golden St. John's wort

Quite a bit of superstition, folklore, and poetry cluster about the multiple varieties of St. John's wort. One species of *Hypericum*, *H. perforatum*, is currently popular for treating anxiety and emotional disturbances, and the legends regarding this shrubby herb go back to the Greeks. Note that the garden shrub discussed here, *H. frondosum*, is in fact listed as a poisonous plant and should never be ingested.

The bright golden yellow, 2-inch (5cm) flowers of this deciduous shrub bring cheery color from midsummer to early autumn. The genus' common name derives from the fact that the flowers are traditionally gathered on June 24th, St. John's Day, but the flowers of golden St. John's wort tend to begin blooming a bit later. Bark is reddish and peeling, ornamented with long, blue-green leaves.

Golden St. John's wort is very easy to grow in most garden soils, including heavy, sometimes dryish, soil with a pH range from 5.0 to 7.5. This shrub will fare well in light shade, though it prefers full sun.

Ilex verticillata

Winterberry

BLOOM TIME: winter–early spring (berries)

HEIGHT/WIDTH: varies 4'–20' × 4'–20' (1.2–6 × 1.2–6m)

LIGHT: full sun–light shade

ZONES: 4–8

OTHER: attracts birds

Winterberry

Birds flock to the winter and spring red fruit of this deciduous hardy native holly, an ideal shrub for wet, almost swampy gardens. In dryer soils, the shrub will still perform well, but will never grow as tall, often a plus in normal garden situations.

You'll want to use the taller varieties, such as the 20-foot (6m) high 'Emily Brunner', if you are planting winterberry as a background; make sure it is accompanied by its pollinator 'James Swan'. For fruit production, all winterberries require both male and female plants to be present. Be clear about this when purchasing, and make sure you get some of each.

Though winterberry drops its deep green leaves in autumn, the smooth, dark branches and bright red berries remain attractive throughout the winter. The branches are often cut and brought indoors for Christmas decorations.

There are at least four hundred species of holly trees, and many more named cultivars. Don't eat any of the berries, which may cause illness. Christmas lore about hollies is plentiful, including the belief that if "He Holly" (from a male plant) is clipped and brought into the house, the husband will be boss for the next year, while if "She Holly" is used for ornament, the wife will rule until the next Christmas. Decorate with a tad of both.

Indigofera kirilowii

Kirilow indigo

BLOOM TIME: summer–autumn

HEIGHT/WIDTH: 5' × 5' (1.5 × 1.5m)

LIGHT: full sun

ZONES: 4–8

Kirilow indigo

If summers are hot where you live, Kirilow indigo proves to be a quite long-flowering shrub, blooming with small, sweet-smelling, pink flowers held in erect racemes from summer through early autumn. The foliage is bright green and the small, fine leaves are somewhat fernlike.

While 5-foot (1.5m) heights are standard, this shrub may grow taller against a warm wall or sunlit fence. Particularly suited for well-drained garden areas that get semiregular watering, Kirilow indigo may be planted either in spring or in autumn. You can multiply Kirilow indigo via root or semi-ripe cuttings.

You may want to shape your shrub, but pruning is generally not necessary. Some gardeners cut it back sharply in spring or autumn when the shrub is dormant in order to produce a bushier growth.

The related species *Indigo amblyantha*, which bears rose or deep pink flowers, is especially hardy. While *I. heterantha* or "false indigo" is less hardy, it does have darker rosy purple flowers. If you need a nitrogen-fixing plant, indigo meets the requirement.

Ixora coccinea

Flame-of-the-woods

BLOOM TIME: late spring–autumn

HEIGHT/WIDTH: 8' × 6' (2.5 × 2m)

LIGHT: full sun

ZONES: 9-10

Flame-of-the-woods

Flame-of-the-woods hails from tropical climes, where its fragrant, bouquet-style, yellow, orange, pink, white, or red flower groupings are almost taken for granted in the consistently warm, humid weather. It's true that this shrub may be a smidge fussy about its growing medium and location, but its blooms are quite spectacular. It requires well-drained, amply organic soil tending toward acidic. Regular watering is an absolute must.

Except for southern Florida and similar climates, flame-of-the-woods is most successfully grown in a greenhouse. If the temperature drops below 59°F (15°C), this warm-climate plant may promptly die back. But don't give up hope too quickly, as it often returns.

Keep a watchful eye out for scale insects and aphids, which will make the leathery, dark green leaves start to yellow. Is flame-of-the-woods really worth all the effort? Yes!

Jasminum nudiflorum

Winter jasmine

BLOOM TIME: midwinter–early spring

HEIGHT/WIDTH: 3' × 5' (1 × 1.5m)

LIGHT: full sun–partial shade

ZONES: 6–9

Winter jasmine

A native of China, winter jasmine needs fertile, well-drained soil, but does well in northern gardens, where other jasmines may prove difficult. Do not anticipate the renowned jasmine fragrance, as the 1-inch (2.5cm) -wide, bright yellow flowers are definitely unscented. Nonetheless, they're a welcome sight in midwinter when any color is a joyful harbinger of the coming warm weather. In really cold weather, the flowers may even freeze. Trifoliate leaves a deep glossy green appear after the flowers on year-old willowy stems. Among the leaves are tiny black berries.

Used as a medium-height shrub or 15-foot (4.5m) -high vine, this rapidly growing jasmine also makes a good deciduous bank cover, rooting wherever draping stems touch soil. Prune winter jasmine occasionally to keep its size and shape appropriate to its site, but make sure to prune after flowering. If old branches seem to have stopped flowering, cut them back severely to assure new growth.

Kalmia latifolia

Mountain laurel

BLOOM TIME: spring

HEIGHT/WIDTH: $10' \times 8'$ (3×2.5m)

LIGHT: partial shade

ZONES: 5–8

OTHER: decorative branches

Mountain laurel

Growing primarily in the woodlands of the East, mountain laurel has glorious white, pink, or red bell-shaped flowers appearing in abundant 6-inch (15cm) -wide clusters. Like azaleas, mountain laurel needs cool, moist, acidic, well-drained soil in order to flourish. As their native habitat would indicate, mountain laurel does well, and looks completely natural, at the edge of a woodland garden. It is also a welcome addition to the shrub border or as part of a foundation planting.

Seed capsules are produced after the flowers pass, but if you want to ensure generous flowering the next season, it is best to remove these capsules. Be aware that leaves and flower nectar are poisonous if ingested. Mountain laurel does grow slowly, but feeding it an azalea-rhododendron fertilizer abets progress. Proper conditions, including a deep mulch, help to ward off occasional localized leaf spot fungus problems.

As a gnarled senior plant, mountain laurel becomes quite picturesque. Native Americans once made spoons from its hard wood; early colonists used it to make weaver's shuttles.

The cultivar 'Heart of Fire' is more adaptable than other cultivars.

Kerria japonica

Japanese kerria

BLOOM TIME: spring–summer, possibly autumn

HEIGHT/WIDTH: 5' × 6' (1.5 × 1.8m)

LIGHT: full sun–partial shade

ZONES: 4–9

'Pleniflora' Japanese kerria

Kerrias tolerate air pollution, and so make excellent plants for industrialized areas. Site these upright-growing shrubs singly or in groups, perhaps mixed with other shrubs for color contrast. Single or double bright golden yellow flowers resembling small wild roses appear on Japanese kerria between May and June, but may make a second showing in autumn. While the single-flowered forms are less hardy than the double-flowered ones, the single will flower quite happily in deep shade. Bright green glossy leaves also turn golden yellow in autumn, prolonging sunny color in the garden.

Flowers are followed by hard, black-brown, inedible fruits, each about 4 inches (10cm) long. Fruits, each containing four to six brownish yellow seeds, ripen in September. Not a fussy shrub, Japanese kerria does well with regular watering and ordinary garden soil. Cut off suckers as necessary.

Several good cultivars offer more options: 'Aureo-vittata' has arching branches that are striped yellow and green, a lively sight in winter; 'Pleniflora' has fully double flowers and is more likely to survive the cold than some other forms.

Kolkwitzia amablis

Beauty bush

BLOOM TIME: late spring–midsummer

HEIGHT/WIDTH: 10' × 8' (3 × 2.5m)

LIGHT: full sun–light shade

ZONES: 5–9

Beauty bush

An abundance of small, bell-shaped flowers carried in 3-inch (7cm) -wide clusters covers this large shrub in early summer. The pale pink flowers have yellow centers, though occasionally the flowers can be found in white or dark pink. Bristly pinkish brown seedpods appear in summer after the flowers, providing interest for an additional few weeks.

Native to China and virtually care-free, this deciduous, hardy plant adapts to many soil types, including lime, and survives a large climate variation. If you place beauty bush in the sun, the dark, gray-green foliage becomes denser and the shrub grows in a more compact shape. Give it semi-shade, and beauty bush's growth is taller and arching, making its delicate, brown, flaking bark more visible in winter.

Wood from the prior year carries the spring flowers, so be judicious when pruning to shape. Occasionally suckers may appear; take them out unless you want the shrub to spread.

Good cultivars to look for include the rosy red 'Rosea' and the deep pink 'Pink Cloud'.

Lagerstroemia indica

Crape myrtle

BLOOM TIME: summer–autumn

HEIGHT/WIDTH: 20' × 10' (6 × 3m)

LIGHT: full sun

ZONES: 7–10

OTHER: attracts birds

Crape myrtle

Crape myrtle's fantastic exfoliating bark is a visual delight, so make sure to place it in the garden where it can be easily appreciated. In fact, horticultural experts consider this deciduous shrub a must for the complete Southern garden.

But there are rewards other than the peeling brown-gray bark, such as dark green leaves that turn to bronze, russet, or red in autumn and an array of flower hues. The flowers of crape myrtle arrive in small, crinkled-petal clusters and they may be as long as 8 inches (20cm). Popular hybrid varieties include the coral-pink 'Comanche',

lavender 'Lipan', and dwarf 'Victor', which has bright red flowers and is perfect for the patio pot or border.

Not fussy as to soil type or pH, crape myrtle does need good drainage. Mulching is beneficial. Plant only container-grown or balled and burlapped plants, as crape myrtle may have some difficulty establishing if planted as a bareroot. This shrub can also be pruned into a small tree. Prune in late winter; flowers are carried on new wood, so pruning will not interfere with bloom.

Lavandula angustifolia

English lavender

BLOOM TIME: summer

HEIGHT/WIDTH: 3' × 3'–4' (1 × 1–1.2m)

LIGHT: full sun

ZONES: 5–8

OTHER: attracts honeybees; good for drying

English lavender

Back when good folk thought baths weren't healthy, something was needed to mask unpleasant body aromas. Evergreen lavender, quite commonly grown, proved to be one solution, as it could be used to make an inexpensive perfume. It is still used in perfume today, as well as in potpourri, soaps, sachets, candles, and as dried scented flower wands.

A favorite for perennial and herb gardens, English lavender has small flowers that appear on long, wiry stems. Often planted along paths, where its glorious scent will be truly appreciated, lavender also makes a good low hedge.

Grow this hardiest of shrubby herbs in dryish, rather limey soil and bright sunshine. It's fine in coastal areas, but absolutely won't tolerate humidity. Deadheading the faded flowers will help assure vigorous new growth.

Varieties include the white-flowered 'Alba', at 3-feet (30cm) tall; 'Twickel Purple', at 18 inches (45cm) tall, with light purple flowers; and 'Irene Doyle' with lavender-blue flowers. For patio or balcony, try the compact 'Rosea' or 'Jean Davis', both with pink flowers. All have serene gray or gray-green leaves.

Lespedeza spp.

Bush clover

BLOOM TIME: early autumn

HEIGHT/WIDTH: 4'–8' × 10' (1.2–2.5 × 3m)

LIGHT: full sun

ZONES: 4–8

Bush clover

Silky, ½-inch (1cm) flowers similar to those of the pea plant create seemingly endless wands of rose-purple on this deciduous shrub. Thriving in areas ranging from rocky outcrops to meadows, this Asian native needs only well-drained, fertile, light soil and full sun.

It's not always easy to find late-flowering, medium-sized shrubs to balance out the garden, but two species of bush clover fit the bill. Shrub bush clover (*Lespedeza bicolor*) has mid- to dark green oval leaves and is somewhat hardier (to Zone 4), while purple bush clover (*L. thunbergii*) has blue-green leaves and is hardy to Zone 5; both have rose-purple flower clusters that reach 6 inches (15cm) or longer. There is also a slightly shorter bush clover cultivar, *L. bicolor* 'Gibralter' with rose-pink flowers, ideal for today's often smaller garden.

Some pests and diseases may annoy this shrub—mainly rust, powdery mildew, and leafhoppers—but good care keeps these to a minimum.

Leucothoe fontanesiana

(L. catasbaei)

Drooping leucothoe

BLOOM TIME: early summer

HEIGHT/WIDTH: 6' × 4' (1.8 × 1.2m)

LIGHT: partial shade–full shade

ZONES: 5–8

'Rainbow' drooping leucothoe

Native to the Southern mountain streamsides of North America, drooping leucothoe demands the same type of conditions when planted elsewhere; it requires acidic, moist, well-drained soil high in organic matter, along with ample protection from the wind. Provide the proper environment and this graceful, fountainlike evergreen augments the spring wildflower or woodland garden with pendulous clusters of fragrant, white flowers.

Come autumn and winter, dark green, leathery, lance-shaped, 5-inch (12cm) -long leaves turn red or bronze-purple. The cultivar 'Scarletta', unsurprisingly, has scarlet foliage in spring, which gradually turns dark green over the summer, then burgundy in autumn. While the shrub retains it foliage in mild winters, the leaves may drop if the cold is severe.

Because leucothoe spreads by means of underground runners, it may form a clump if its conditions are good. Suitable companion plants for leucothoe include mountain laurel, azaleas, and rhododendrons.

There's also a dwarf variety, at 3 feet (1m) high, called 'Rainbow' (also sometimes called 'Girard's Rainbow'), which has red, yellow, and cream variegated foliage.

Ligustrum spp.

Privet

BLOOM TIME: midsummer

HEIGHT/WIDTH: 10' (3m) × varies widely

LIGHT: full sun–partial shade

ZONES: 4–9

OTHER: attracts birds, honeybees, butterflies

English privet

All privets are used extensively as clipped or unclipped hedging shrubs, and make worthy specimens as well. When the shrubs are clipped they do not produce flowers or berries, but left to their natural shape the plants produce small but attractive white flowers in midsummer. Very hard, shiny, black berries appear after flowers have passed.

Privets—grown mainly for their green, glossy, oval leaves—are admired as tough, quick-growing shrubs. They are tolerant of a wide range of conditions, including the challenges of city gardens. Except for English, or common,

privet, which is subject to blight in some areas, they are generally free of pests and diseases. Note that ingestion of any part of the privet plant will cause serious illness.

English privet (*L. vulgare*), is a wide-growing shrub that is usually deciduous but may remain semievergreen in the South. Ibolium privet (*L. × ibolium*), an upright-growing deciduous shrub, is one of the prettiest privets for more northern climes (to Zone 5), and closely resembles California privet (*L. ovalifolium*), a beautiful choice for Zone 6 and southward.

Lindera benzoin

Spice bush

BLOOM TIME: spring

HEIGHT/WIDTH: 10' × 6' (3 × 1.8m)

LIGHT: partial shade

ZONES: 5–9

OTHER: attracts honeybees, birds

Spice bush

Spice is nice, especially when it occurs in fragrant flowers, twigs, and foliage. In fact, the twigs and leaves were once used to flavor food and teas. This eastern North American native develops masses of small yellow flowers that appear while branches are still bare. Large medium green leaves cover the shrub when flowers have finished. In autumn, the leaves turn yellow and frame ½-inch (1cm) red fruits. Early American colonists sometimes dried the fruits, then ground them into a powder as a substitute for allspice. Fruiting occurs on female plants only if there's a male spice bush in the vicinity, so keep this in mind when planning your garden.

Make sure to buy container-grown or balled and burlapped shrubs, as bareroot spice bush is difficult to get established. Plant spice bush in acidic, moist, well-drained soil, and don't plan on moving it. Transplanting can be difficult due to an extended, deep, root system. You'll want to encourage a profusion of wildflowers in the vicinity, as they bloom just about the same time as spice bush, a double treat.

Lonicera fragrantissima

Fragrant honeysuckle

BLOOM TIME: late winter–early spring

HEIGHT/WIDTH: 6' × 6' (1.8 × 1.8m)

LIGHT: full sun–partial shade

ZONES: 5–8

OTHER: attracts honeybees, hummingbirds, birds

Fragrant honeysuckle

To recall soft memories of childhood spring evenings, cradle a honeysuckle blossom in your hand and inhale deeply. Even just one creamy-white, ½-inch (1cm) flower is a fragrant gem—an entire shrub can be nostalgic nirvana. Leaves are bluish green and delicate red berries succeed flowers, though they are often stolen by birds as soon as they ripen. Note that the berries are not edible by humans, and can cause illness.

Named after a German physician, Adam Lonicer, this hearty shrub may even be trained as a multistemmed small tree. Tolerating a variety of soils, fragrant honeysuckle requires only moderate water. Site this semievergreen winner where its glorious scent can be best enjoyed, but note that it is wide-spreading, and may have to be constantly pruned if not given enough room. Make sure to prune after flowering, as blooms are carried on the previous year's wood. Full sun is best, but fragrant honeysuckle will tolerate some shade, while continuing to flower.

There are many honeysuckle species and cultivars, and not all are fragrant. Scented shrub alternatives are *Lonicera syringantha*, which bears lilac flowers, and *L. standishii*, which has white flowers.

Magnolia stellata

Star magnolia

BLOOM TIME: late winter–early spring

HEIGHT/WIDTH: 8' × 8' (2.5 × 2.5m)

LIGHT: full sun–light shade

ZONES: 5–9

OTHER: good cut flowers for fragrance

Star magnolia

Many think sweet-scented magnolias exist solely in huge tree form, but deciduous shrub forms abound, including the 8-foot (2.4m) -tall *Magnolia stellata* 'Royal Star' and *M. stellata* 'Waterlily', as well as *M. sieboldii* 'Siebold', and *M.* 'Jane', which may grow to 15 feet (4.5m) tall. Many magnolias may be grown either as multistemmed shrubs or as single-stem small trees.

Flower colors may vary: 'Jane' bears 3-inch (7cm) flowers that are reddish purple outside and white inside; 'Waterlily' has pink buds and white flowers tinged with pink; and 'Siebold' has brilliant red stamens that ornament white, cup-shaped flowers. Most magnolias are fairly hardy, but do need moist, organic, well-drained, lime-free soil in order to thrive. Just place them in an uncrowded site where they are to remain, then enjoy ample flowers in early spring. When planted in a sheltered spot, magnolias may bloom earlier than they otherwise would, star magnolia being among the earliest to bloom. Cut flowers, placed in ornamental bowls, both perfume and decorate a room.

Mahonia aquifolium

Oregon grapeholly

BLOOM TIME: spring

HEIGHT/WIDTH: 3' × 5' (1 × 1.5m)

LIGHT: partial shade–shade

ZONES: 5–9

OTHER: attracts birds

Oregon grapeholly

Native to North America, Oregon grapeholly's common name derives from its region of origin, its grapelike clusters of dark blue berries, and its shiny, green, hollylike leaves. Seasonal changes serve Oregon grapeholly well. In spring, small, golden-yellow flowers are carried in dense, upright, 3-inch (8cm) -long racemes. The glaucous berries ripen in autumn, and the stiff glossy leaves turn reddish bronze in winter.

This evergreen shrub thrives in moist, well-drained, slightly acidic soil that is high in organic matter. Generally hardy, it requires protection from both wind and very hot sun. Oregon grapeholly combines well with conifers, makes a fine low hedge, and does well as an underplanting beneath large trees. The shrub spreads by underground stems, and may form large clumps over time.

There is a shorter version, 'Compacta', which reaches to only 3 feet (90cm) in height; it has yellow flowers but bears few fruits.

Malus sargentii

Sargent crabapple

BLOOM TIME: late spring

HEIGHT/WIDTH: 6' × 12' (1.8 × 3.5m)

LIGHT: full sun

ZONES: 4–8

OTHER: attracts birds

Sargent crabapple

Most of the twenty-five crabapple species are trees, but a few have the compact, mounding habit that qualifies them as shrubs. Native to Asia, Sargent crabapple grows wider than it does tall, and has a horizontal branching habit. Sargent crabapple wins accolades not only for its musky-sweet scent, showy white flower clusters, profuse dark red fruits, and leaves that turn orange and yellow in autumn, but also for its superb disease resistance. Unlike most other crabapples, Sargent crabapple is not susceptible to cedar-apple rust.

Like all crabapples, it requires regular watering and tolerates most soils, as long as they are well-drained. It does not tolerate shade, however. Remember that for this species, sun equals flowers. The flowers are followed by pea-sized fruits, which will display through most of the winter if not eaten by birds.

The cultivar 'Rosea' has pink flowers; 'Candymint' bears lovely pink flowers with red borders.

Myrtus communis

Common myrtle

BLOOM TIME: spring–autumn

HEIGHT/WIDTH: 3' × 3' (1 × 1m)

LIGHT: full sun

ZONES: 8–9

OTHER: bonsai

Common myrtle

In European folklore, myrtle brings happiness to the house it surrounds. Bridal bouquets often contained fragrant myrtle sprigs, which were later planted close to the door of a new home, and it was one of the plants the ancient Greeks used to make crowns for celebrated figures. Cultivated for its aromatic, glossy, green leaves as well as its sweet-smelling, cream-colored flowers, this evergreen needs well-drained soil, but tolerates both heat and occasional drought.

White berries follow the fragrant flowers. While *Myrtus communis*, common myrtle, gets rather tall, there are multi-ple shorter varieties: *M. communis* 'Compacta' stays at 3 feet (90cm) tall and makes a good low hedging shrub, as do the slightly taller cultivars 'Jenny Reitenbach' and 'Nana'.

While myrtle will not survive the winter in regions above Zone 8, it is perfect for growing in containers and moving indoors for the winter. All myrtles make fine topiary plants for yard or patio, and the smaller ones can be trained for bonsai.

Nandina domestica

Heavenly bamboo

BLOOM TIME: midsummer

HEIGHT/WIDTH: 6' × 3' (1.8 × 1m)

LIGHT: full sun–partial shade

ZONES: 6–9

Heavenly bamboo

The word "bamboo" may conjure in the minds of gardeners images of underground rhizomes taking over a yard. But don't let this nickname, a misnomer, scare you away from the self-contained, beautifully textured *Nandina*, actually not a bamboo at all. Heavenly bamboo is not particular about soil, though semimoist soil is best; the plant is practically pest-free.

In midsummer, small, clustered, white flowers appear in profusion. Throughout the year, heavenly bamboo's fine foliage is a beautiful asset, but it really shines in autumn, when the leaves turn brilliant red and bronze. Large clusters of dark orange-red fruit in autumn create a festive holiday garden appearance.

In the northern reaches of its zone, heavenly bamboo will benefit from some winter protection, and even then may succumb to severe winters.

A favorite in Japanese gardens, heavenly bamboo may also be planted in hedges or as a graceful specimen planting.

For even more color, try the cultivar 'Yellow Fruited'. Patio varieties, such as the 2-foot (60cm) -high 'Fire Power', are also available.

Nerium oleander

Oleander

BLOOM TIME: late spring–autumn

HEIGHT/WIDTH: varies widely

LIGHT: full sun

ZONES: 8-9

Oleander

This shrub is so durable and easy to grow, it is planted along freeways in several states. In the garden, it does require caution, since all parts are poisonous if ingested. In fact, wood must not be used for barbecue or other food skewers, or burnt where smoke can be inhaled. Yet for tough garden sections, oleander survives where other plants fail. In addition to tolerating auto exhaust fumes, the shrub withstands somewhat salty soil and partial drought.

Beautifully ornamental, this warm-climate shrub produces clusters of red, pink, or white flowers from spring until autumn. The foliage, too, is attractive, and remains green throughout the seasons.

Oleander's size varies widely, from 'Petite Pink', which reaches only 3 feet (1m) in height, to the white-flowered 'Sister Agnes', which can grow moderately quickly to 20 feet (6m) tall. Make certain to ask the nursery about the ultimate size of the cultivar you wish to purchase. Since there are multiple color choices, including apricot, lilac, yellow, and several reds, seeing this evergreen shrub in bloom before purchasing is a good idea.

Osmanthus heterophyllus

Holly osmanthus

BLOOM TIME: autumn

HEIGHT/WIDTH: 10' × 10' (3 × 3m)

LIGHT: full sun–partial shade

ZONES: 6–9

'Goshiki' holly osmanthus

Autumn bloom makes this an excellent shrub for the year-round garden. While the quite small, white, tubular flower clusters aren't easily visible among the dark, glossy, holly-like, evergreen leaves, their presence becomes obvious once you sniff the extremely sweet fragrance. Specimen planting is always recommended near a window where the fragrance can be thoroughly enjoyed. Holly osmanthus is also quite useful as a dense barrier hedge.

Moderately hardy, holly osmanthus needs moist, well-drained, somewhat acidic soil, and protection from cold, strong winds. Purple-black fruits appear only in warm areas. This useful shrub performs quite well both in sun and shade, which makes it a versatile plant for foundation plantings or for hedging. Hard pruning won't harm the shrub; prune in early spring.

There are several good cultivars available, including 'Goshiki', which has bronze-tinted leaves in spring, later splashed with yellow; 'Variegatus', which has cream-edged leaves; and 'Purpureus', which has unusual, deep purple new leaves in spring.

Paeonia suffruticosa

Tree peony

BLOOM TIME: spring

HEIGHT/WIDTH: 6' × 6' (1.8 × 1.8m)

LIGHT: mild sun–partial shade

ZONES: 4–8

Tree peony

Regarded as the "King of Flowers" by the Chinese, the tree peony's extraordinarily showy, fragrant, large flowers have made this plant prized in horticultural circles for centuries. Chinese writings more than eight hundred years old record peony collections, one enthusiast growing as many as sixty thousand peonies. While most people are familiar with the popular herbaceous peonies (*Paeonia lactiflora*), not all are aware of the deciduous shrubs discussed here.

If given a satisfactory environment, the beautiful tree peony is not difficult to grow. It needs rich, somewhat moist, well-drained soil with morning sun and afternoon shade. It does not tolerate soggy soil, strong winds, or being disturbed. Prune tree peony in spring, after it flowers. Container-grown or balled and burlapped plants may be set out at any time during the year. Bareroot tree peonies must be planted in autumn.

Gorgeous new color selections are available each year. 'Karmada Fuji' is a semidouble lavender pink. 'Demetra' is a double yellow-gold, with petals edged in burgundy. 'Hyphestos' is a double-flowered dark red with pointed, ruffled petals.

Philadelphus coronarius

Fragrant mock orange

BLOOM TIME: early summer

HEIGHT/WIDTH: 8' × 7' (2.5 × 2m)

LIGHT: full sun–partial shade

ZONES: 5–8

OTHER: attracts butterflies, honeybees

Fragrant mock orange

The enchanting orange blossom fragrance of this serene shrub transforms it from Cinderella plainness into a garden princess. It almost seems a miracle that such ordinary green leaves and unprepossessing white flowers can scent the air with romance on a fine spring day.

The upright-growing deciduous mock orange accomplishes all this without requiring much effort from the gardener. It grows in any garden soil, seldom gets serious pests or diseases, and you won't have to worry about constant watering, as mock orange tolerates occasional drought.

Mock orange grows well in full sun or in light shade. Fragrant mock orange is among the hardiest of the mock oranges, and when in a sheltered spot may survive winters even in the southern ranges of Zone 4, though it is reliably hardy to Zone 5. Select your specimens when they are in bloom, as some plants have the mock orange label, but lack the fragrance.

If you are planting for porch or patio, look for the cultivar 'Dwarf Snowflake', which reaches only 3 feet (1m) in height.

Photonia fraseri

Fraser photonia

BLOOM TIME: spring

HEIGHT/WIDTH: 15' × 15' (4.5 × 4.5m)

LIGHT: full sun

ZONES: 7–9

OTHER: branches good for arranging

Fraser photonia

A good accent plant because of its bright, bronze-red, springtime foliage, Fraser photinia's leaves mature to a deep green. Small, ivory-colored flower clusters that appear in midspring, followed by red berries, complete the show.

Vigorous and fast-growing photonia requires full sun and a well-drained soil with ample organic matter. The soil should be improved with peat moss or leaf mold when the shrubs are planted and on a continuing basis. Water Fraser photinia profusely, aiming at roots rather than leaves, to forestall fireblight problems. In the northern parts of photonia's hardiness range, cut back watering in autumn to allow the leaves to mature before winter sets in. Aphids and scale insects can also present problems.

Fraser photonia does well in containers, so consider it for patio use. It also makes an unusual espalier, an eye-catching hedge, and a tidy small tree. Pruning is the key to getting the desired shape.

Popular cultivars available include 'Red Robin', 'Birmingham', and the very vigorous 'Robusta'.

Pieris floribunda

Mountain andromeda, mountain pieris

BLOOM TIME: spring

HEIGHT/WIDTH: 6' × 6' (1.8 × 1.8m)

LIGHT: partial shade

ZONES: 5–8

Mountain andromeda

While less widely available than *Pieris japonica*, this broad-leaved evergreen pieris has a better resistance to lacebug and a higher pH tolerance, so it's worth checking specialty nurseries and mail-order sources to find this species. Upright 5-inch (13cm) -long clusters of tiny, fragrant, white flowers display themselves in spring among fine-textured, deep green leaves that make their initial appearance with red-bronze coloration. If ingested, leaves may cause severe discomfort. In late summer, buds form for the following year's flowers, and remain decorative through the autumn and winter.

Native to southeastern North America's damp mountain slopes, mountain andromeda prefers cool, moist, somewhat acidic soil, plus shelter from wind, cold, and harsh winter sun. A sheltered situation, perhaps against the wall of a house, is especially important in the northern reaches of the shrub's hardiness range. Once established and given a mulch, mountain andromeda is drought-tolerant, barring extremely hot weather. A slow-grower, this gracefully arching shrub is ideal for smaller gardens and looks particularly beautiful when combined with needleleaf evergreens.

Pittosporum tobira

Japanese pittosporum

BLOOM TIME: spring

HEIGHT/WIDTH: 15' × 12' (4.5 × 3.5m)

LIGHT: full sun–partial shade

ZONES: 9–10

'Variegata' Japanese pittosporum

Flowers with the fragrance of orange blossoms make Japanese pittosporum a prized addition to the scented garden. Pittosporum's small, creamy white flowers appear in multiple clusters among dark green, leathery leaves. Leaves are spaced quite close together on the stems, and appear to grow in whorls. Flowers are followed by pear-shaped, yellow-brown seed capsules that split open in autumn, displaying red-orange seeds. The vigorous growing habit, mild watering needs, and low maintenance of this popular ever-green shrub make it useful for foundation plantings, screens, and borders. Prune lightly only as necessary. Japanese pittosporum will grow in nearly any soil, and adapts to heat and to the windy conditions of the coast. The species will also tolerate some shade. For the patio garden, Japanese pittosporum does well in containers, and can be trained as a small, crooked-stemmed tree.

The cultivar 'Variegata' has gray-green leaves edged with white.

Plumbago auriculata

Cape plumbago

BLOOM TIME: spring–autumn

HEIGHT/WIDTH: 10'–20' × 3'–10' (3–6 × 1–3m)

LIGHT: full sun

ZONES: 9–10

Cape plumbago

Grow cape plumbago as a shrub or as a vine, and enjoy pale blue or white (*Plumbago auriculata* var. *alba*), 1-inch (2.5cm) -wide flowers grouped in clusters up to 4 inches (10cm) wide. Flowers, which are surrounded by light green leaves, may continue to bloom throughout the year in climates that get no frost. Persuade free-flowering bloom by giving cape plumbago a sheltered position in full sun and fertile soil.

This South African native semievergreen has many roles, including a drought-tolerant one. Give it well-drained soil and only occasional water once established. A feisty sprawler, cape plumbago takes its time at the starting gate, but once it gets going, it will cover a fence or an otherwise dismal hillock. Fertilize cape plumbago in early spring and again in midsummer to stimulate growth. Pinch off the tips of long young canes to encourage branching. Unless you desire a very large shrub, cut old canes back to the ground each spring. Make sure to use gloves, as handling the plant may cause severe skin irritation.

Potentilla fruticosa

Bush cinquefoil

BLOOM TIME: late spring–autumn

HEIGHT/WIDTH: 4' × 4' (1.2 × 1.2m)

LIGHT: full sun

ZONES: 2–7

Bush cinquefoil

The fine-textured, grayish green foliage on this dense, bushy shrub makes a complementary backdrop for colorful annuals and perennials. The common name "cinquefoil" derives from the shrub's five-fingered leaf, a popular emblem of long-ago heraldry; it symbolized the five senses and fivefold victory. Single yellow flowers, about 1 inch (2.5cm) wide, appear profusely in midsummer and may continue until frost.

Incredibly easy to grow, bush cinquefoil needs only a sunny spot in well-drained soil. This upright-growing shrub is bothered by no pests or diseases and needs no pruning. Use bush cinquefoil in hedges, as specimens, or in a shrub border.

Good cultivars of bush cinquefoil abound, with many different color selections, including 'Tangerine', with copper-colored flowers; 'Abbotswood' with white blooms; 'Day Dawn', which bears pale pink flowers; 'Red Ace', a red with yellow centers; and the new double-flowered 'Yellowbird'. Note that with brighter red, orange, or yellow flowers fading from the sun may occur.

Prunus glandulosa

Chinese bush cherry

BLOOM TIME: April

HEIGHT/WIDTH: 4' × 5' (1.2 × 1.5m)

LIGHT: full sun

ZONES: 5–8

OTHER: attracts honeybees

Chinese bush cherry

If you need a small shrub, this hardy ornamental cherry is among the most widely cultivated of the two hundred *Prunus* species due to its profuse early bloom. Slender bare branches are almost completely covered by clusters of splendidly small blooms in white or pink. The flowers, which may come in both single and double forms, are soon joined by ovoid, medium green leaves. Tiny, dark red berries appear on single-flowered forms only, after flowers have passed. Ingestion of either leaves or fruit causes severe discomfort.

All *Prunus* species thrive in ordinary garden soil, doing best in a reasonably wind-free site. They also need full sun. Regular, modest fertilization is beneficial.

For those interested in re-creating a Victorian or Edwardian garden of ages past, consider *Prunus glandulosa* 'Sinensis'. Its bright pink double flowers made this shrub very popular during those decorative days, and it appeared in thousands of gardens across England and North America.

Prunus triloba

Flowering almond

BLOOM TIME: early spring

HEIGHT/WIDTH: 8' × 8' (2.5 × 2.5m)

LIGHT: full sun

ZONES: 6–8

OTHER: attracts honeybees

Flowering almond

Flowering almond is a delightful ornamental rather than a delicious almond-provider, and can be pruned to make a small tree as well as left to form a substantial dense shrub. Peach-pink, many-petaled double flowers, each about 1½ inches (3.5cm) across, resemble small rose. There is also a single-flowered form. The blooms herald springtime along the length of long, narrow branches. Round red fruits, which may cause severe discomfort if eaten, follow the flowers.

Use this shrub in hedges, in a shrub border, or against a wall. The darker the wall, the better the pink blossoms display. While hedges need to be trimmed after flowering, this very durable deciduous shrub doesn't otherwise require a lot of care if sited in a sunny, well-drained area.

Note that the name *Prunus triloba plena* appears in many catalogs to distinguish the double-flowered forms from the single-flowered ones, but this designation has no botanical standing. The shrub is in fact the same species as *Prunus triloba*. The cultivar 'Multiplex' flowers in midspring.

Punica granatum

Pomegranate

BLOOM TIME: summer–early autumn

HEIGHT/WIDTH: 10' × 7' (3 × 2m)

LIGHT: full sun

ZONES: 8–10

Pomegranate

Julia Child, empress of delectable cuisine, mentions rolling pomegranate seeds into small cream cheese balls or cooking them to make a delicious jelly. These are just a few ideas in addition to eating them scooped directly from the 3-inch (7cm) -wide red fruit picked right off the tree in autumn. 'Wonderful' is the best fruit-bearing cultivar now available. Fruit follows funnel-shaped, bright orange-red flowers, each over 3 inches (7cm) wide. Double-flowered forms are available, and bloom for several months in summer but do not bear fruit.

In the open garden, pomegranate can be grown as a deciduous shrub or small tree. Plant it in well-drained, average soil, and water regularly. A sunny location is mandatory for fruiting and plant survival, and a hotter, drier climate will stimulate the shrub to produce more fruit. In slow-sun climates, up the odds by placing pomegranate near a heat-reflecting wall. A dwarf variety, 'Nana', which has scarlet flowers, is available, but fruits are small and dry. Make certain the *Punica* you purchase bears edible fruit, if that's your garden hope.

Pyracantha coccinea

Scarlet firethorn

BLOOM TIME: early summer

HEIGHT/WIDTH: 8' × 8' (2.5 × 2.5m)

LIGHT: full sun–light shade

ZONES: 6–9

OTHER: attracts honeybees, birds

Scarlet firethorn

The botanical name of this popular shrub comes from the Greek words *pyr*, meaning fire, and *akanthos*, meaning thorn—an apt name. Long thorns are piercing and plentiful, so place this shrub away from pathways and make sure it has ample space to spread. Pruning is beneficial, but use long cutting tools or protective garden gloves. Dryish soil and full sun are best for this thorny shrub.

Small, creamy white flowers precede ample clusters of bright scarlet, pea-sized berries. Berries appear in autumn and would probably persist into midwinter except that birds eat them with a voracious appetite.

Evergreen firethorn is occasionally afflicted with fireblight, which causes blackened leaves almost overnight, although many plants regrow. Otherwise, the shrub is fairly durable. *Pyracantha coccinea* is less affected by fireblight than some other species, and the cultivar 'Mohave' has been bred for resistance to both scab and fireblight.

The cultivar 'Lalandii', with orange berries, is more cold-tolerant than the species; 'Harlequin' has variegated leaves rather than the usual dark green.

Rhamnus frangula

Alder buckthorn

BLOOM TIME: summer

HEIGHT/WIDTH: 15' × 12' (4.5 × 3.5m)

LIGHT: full sun

ZONES: 2–8

OTHER: attracts honeybees

Alder buckthorn

This is the only buckthorn with autumn color, its dark green glossy leaves turning bright red or yellow in autumn. Despite its name, this large shrub has no thorns.

Flowers are tiny, whitish green, and appear in clusters. Small berries follow the flowers, and ripen from green to yellow to red to black. Ingestion of leaves, bark, or fruit causes severe discomfort. Give this very hardy shrub moist, organic, slightly acidic soil and full sun. It is tolerant of air pollution, and will grown even in very wet soils. If pruning is necessary to shape or to curtail size, clip the shrub in early spring.

While not an otherwise demonstrative shrub, the cultivar 'Columnaris' has ample virtue as a hedging or screening plant, making a dense barrier that requires minimal trimming. 'Aspenifolia', otherwise known as fern-leaf buckthorn, doesn't have the red-to-black small berries of the species and 'Columnaris', however it does have very long, narrow, glossy leaves that give it a lacy demeanor.

Rhaphiolepis umbellata

Yeddo hawthorn

BLOOM TIME: summer (cool climates); winter–late spring (hot climates)

HEIGHT/WIDTH: 4' × 5' (1.2 × 1.5m)

LIGHT: full sun–partial shade

ZONES: 8–10

Yeddo hawthorn

This vigorous white-flowering shrub can be planted as a specimen, as a formal or informal low hedge, or in mixed borders for flower diversity. It can even be potted up in a container for the patio or balcony. Purple-black berries appear in spring, along with new leaves shaded bronze. Mature leaves, 3 inches (7cm) long, are dark green and rounded, with a glossy, leathery texture.

Evergreen Yeddo hawthorn does best in full sun, but tolerates light shade as well. It adapts to a variety of soils, including ocean coast, but requires regular watering in very dry soils, though it will tolerate brief periods of drought. Pests are minimal, but watch out for leaf spot fungi. Plant this shrub in spring or in autumn, and make sure to water well until established.

If you like Yeddo hawthorn, but want a truly compact variety, consider the cultivar called 'Minor'.

Rhododendron calendulaceum

Flame azalea

BLOOM TIME: late spring–early summer

HEIGHT/WIDTH: 10' × 8' (3 × 2.5m)

LIGHT: partial shade

ZONES: 5–9

Flame azalea

Two hundred years ago, a horticultural writer proclaimed flame azalea as "certainly the most gay and brilliant flowering shrub yet known." Azaleas are among the most free-flowering of all deciduous shrubs. Not only are the large, trumpet-shaped flowers vivid shades of red, orange, and yellow, but the autumn leaves often take on the same hues. The blooms last for several weeks, and during that time the woods seem to be on fire with color. While pretty, the leaves are poisonous if ingested.

Less demanding than evergreen rhododendrons, flame azaleas still need moist, well-drained soil with a pH of 5.0 to 6.0. If you live in an area with acidic soil, your flame azaleas will thrive, but if you live in a region with alkaline soil, you will most likely have to treat the soil with an acidifier or replace the soil in which you are to plant your azaleas. In clay soils, it is best to plant in raised beds, where good drainage can be assured. Use a special azalea fertilizer regularly. Plant flame azaleas in late spring or early autumn, and give them a site with some relief from the hot sun—a lightly shaded spot like the edge of a woodland garden is ideal. Native to Eastern North America, flame azaleas should be a definite part of any heirloom garden.

Rhododendron schlippenbachii

Royal azalea

BLOOM TIME: late spring

HEIGHT/WIDTH: 6'–8' × 6'–8' (1.8–2.5 × 1.8–2.5m)

LIGHT: partial shade

ZONES: 5–8

Royal azalea

Buy this deciduous shrub while it is in bloom to find the most satisfying hue for your garden, as it has some color variation, from white to pale pink to deep rose. Trumpet-shaped, 3-inch (7cm) -wide flowers are quite fragrant and are surrounded by dark green leaves, creating small, natural bouquets. Royal azalea's leaves turn a multitude of colors in autumn: red, orange, and yellow. Delightful to look at, ingestion of plant parts can cause serious illness.

Unlike most other rhododendrons, royal azalea does not require highly acidic soil, performing well with a soil pH of about 6.5. However it does demand excellent drainage, as well as protection from wind and high summer heat. A site under a high-branched tree may work well, though you must remember that rhododendrons like ample water and tree roots can be competitive. Don't forget to mulch, which will help the roots stay cool and the soil retain water.

Rhodotypos scandens

Jetbead

BLOOM TIME: late spring–summer

HEIGHT/WIDTH: 5' × 7' (1.5 × 2m)

LIGHT: full sun–partial shade

ZONES: 5–8

Jetbead

Shiny, black, pea-sized fruits arranged in groups of four, ornament this adaptable shrub throughout otherwise drab winter months, giving added interest and depth to the garden scene. In spring 1¼-inch (3cm) -wide, papery white flowers display a clean-cut demeanor amongst dark green 4-inch (10cm) -long, toothed leaves. The flowers persist into midsummer, and are followed by the fruits.

Jetbead, also called "black jetbead," "jetberry bush," and "white kerria" adjusts to just about any garden soil, wet or dry. Not only does it disregard insect pests but it doesn't flinch a bit at air pollution. If pruning is required, clip this shrub in spring. The only cause for hesitation in planting this adaptable flowering shrub are its fruits, which are highly poisonous if eaten. Otherwise, jetbead is an ideal deciduous shrub for small urban or suburban gardens, since it thrives both in sun or partial shade, and stays under 6 feet (1.8m) tall.

Ribes aureum

Golden currant

BLOOM TIME: spring–summer

HEIGHT/WIDTH: 7' × 5' (2 × 1.5m)

LIGHT: full sun

ZONES: 3–8

Golden currant

Drooping clusters of small, tubular, yellow flowers give off a delicious spicy fragrance, and are followed by red, orange, or black fruits. But this medium-sized, leathery-leafed flowering shrub is grown for its ornamental value rather than its fruits. Like the other one hundred and fifty species of *Ribes*, golden currant is usually planted in groups and is used to cover slopes and fill odd spaces in the garden. It also makes a good hedging shrub, either clipped or unclipped.

Of all the currants, hardy golden currants are the best for the novice gardener, as they are forgiving of a number of adverse conditions. Not overly particular as to soil, as long as it's well-drained, deciduous golden currant will succeed in both sandy and gravelly soils as well as good loam. The better the soil, the more the shrub will sucker. Air pollution doesn't affect growth. Cut back old shoots after flowering to stimulate new growth.

Note that currants may carry a fungus, called white pine blister rust, that affects white pines trees; *Ribes* species are therefore prohibited in certain regions. Check with your local agricultural extension office to be sure that any currant you are planning to include in your garden is safe for your area.

Ribes odoratum

Clove currant, buffalo currant

BLOOM TIME: late spring

HEIGHT/WIDTH: 7' × 5' (2 × 1.5m)

LIGHT: partial shade

ZONES: 5–8

OTHER: attracts birds; fruit for preserves

Clove currant

If you make preserves and want to experiment with a scintilla of clove, place clove currant near your kitchen door, where you can garner a few small black fruits with just a step or two outside. The clovelike aroma from sunny yellow flowers is so delightful that you should be certain to site this shrub near a porch, patio, or window if the backdoor entry spot won't do. Just make certain that clove currant's situation is quite dry and somewhat shady, as this deciduous Great Plains native thrives best in its traditional environment. Meet this shrub's needs and you'll get not only edible fruit, perky flowers, and spicy scent, but also pale green leaves that turn a lovely scarlet in autumn. Note that you'll need a plant of each sex in order to produce fruit. Clove currant spreads by means of underground suckers, so make sure to allow it plenty of space.

Like golden currant and other *Ribes* species, clove currant may act as a host for white pine blister rust, a fungus that decimates white pine trees. For this reason, currants' use is restricted in certain regions, so make sure to check with your local agricultural extension agent before planting.

The cultivar 'Crandall' has extra-large fruits, tart and sweet.

Robinia hispida

Rose acacia, bristly locust

BLOOM TIME: late spring–early summer

HEIGHT/WIDTH: 8' × 6' (2.5 × 1.8m)

LIGHT: full sun

ZONES: 6–10

OTHER: attracts honeybees

'Rosea' rose acacia

Pollution- and drought-tolerant, this very tough, thornless, deciduous shrub fits well in semi-wild areas, where its suckering tendencies won't be a nuisance to smaller plants. Small, rose pink flowers similar to those of the pea plant hang in loose clusters about 6 inches (15 cm) long. The large clusters mean that the flowers can be appreciated from some distance, a decided benefit. Blooms are sometimes followed by bristly, brown seedpods. Soft, fine, red bristles cover the stems.

Not at all particular as to soil, rose acacia even tolerates stony and sandy ground, but make sure to plant it in full sun. This vigorous shrub grows at a rate of 12 inches (30cm) or more per year. Young shrubs must be staked, as branches are brittle and will break in the wind. Regular pruning is necessary.

A less commonly seen variety is *Robinia hispida* var. *fertilis*, which has narrower leaves that feature downy undersides.

Rosa rugosa

Japanese rose, sea tomato

BLOOM TIME: spring–autumn

HEIGHT/WIDTH: 6' × 5' (1.8 × 1.5m)

LIGHT: full sun

ZONES: 2–9

OTHER: attracts birds

Japanese rose

Prickly stems make Japanese rose a good barrier shrub as well as a formidable groundcover designed to keep off wanderers. Among the hardiest of roses, this gorgeous wild rose needs little care. Aside from good drainage and lots of sun, its has virtually no requirements. Single, 2-inch (5 cm) -wide, dark green leaves change to orange in autumn, and orange-red fruits, called hips, form. These hips are rich in vitamin C, and have been used to make jellies and herbal teas. They are also a notorious favorite of birds.

In some areas Japanese rose is used as a roadside plant, and it has no problems adapting to ocean salt spray, wind, or hard frosts.

Three of the many excellent cultivars are 'Fru Dagmar Hastrup', which has clove-scented, rose-pink flowers followed by crimson rosehips; 'Blanc Double de Coubert', which bears large, semidouble, fragrant, white flowers and intermittent red rosehips; and 'Roseraie de l'Hay, with double, strongly fragrant, wine-red flowers.

Rosmarinus officinalis

Rosemary

BLOOM TIME: winter–spring

HEIGHT/WIDTH: 2'–6' × 8' (.6–1.8 × 2.5m)

LIGHT: full sun

ZONES: 8–10

OTHER: attracts honeybees

'Blue Spire' rosemary

Bouquets of rosemary were once brought to bridegrooms on a wedding morning, in the hope of assuring a happy marriage. Plant of legend, perfumery, culinary, and medicinal use, the easygoing rosemary does well in poor, albeit well-drained soils. It is most cheerful in sunny areas, but will survive even in ones where light reflects off a wall. Water-thrifty once established, rosemary doesn't have any serious pests, and requires no fertilizer.

Tiny, lavender-blue flowers appear in clusters during winter, a welcome sight, as well as in spring. Needlelike leaves are pungently fragrant when rolled between fingers.

These leaves can be harvested at any time for culinary use, and make a perfect seasoning for chicken, lamb, or potatoes.

While rosemary will not winter outdoors above Zone 8, it is commonly grown in cooler climates in pots and wintered in a sunny spot indoors. The pots can then be moved outside in summer. Rosemary can also be grown as a standard and is a favorite subject for small topiaries.

Choose from a variety of cultivars, including trailing 'Irene'; 2-foot (60cm) -tall and spreading silvery green 'Lockwood'; 'Golden Rain', which has gold-striped needles in spring; and brightly flowered 'Tuscan Blue'.

Rubus odoratus

Flowering raspberry, thimbleberry

BLOOM TIME: summer

HEIGHT/WIDTH: 8' × 10' (2.5 × 3m)

LIGHT: partial shade

ZONES: 7–9

OTHER: attracts birds

Flowering raspberry

This ultra-tough, fast-growing, thornless shrub—native to the eastern part of North America—makes a good thicket in a wild or woodland garden, particularly if allowed to enjoy its suckering habit. Raspberry-scented, rose-purple flowers, up to 2 inches (5cm) wide, appear during the summer and are followed by red, raspberrylike fruits in long-summer zones. Dark to light green leaves are attractive and unusual, being maple-shaped with a velvety texture.

This *Rubus* is grown as an ornamental shrub and does not have edible fruit. If you want the fresh raspberries or blackberries, there are other, equally hardy *Rubus* varieties to choose from. Check a specialty book on growing fruits and berries or ask at your local nursery, as good fruit production requires certain care of the bushes.

Grow flowering raspberry in well-drained, average soil in partial shade. If you must put it in a spot with lots of sun, make sure to keep the soil evenly moist. Note that flowering raspberry spreads aggressively by way of suckers, so don't plant it unless you have the space to give it. Prune hard to promote flowering.

There are several good cultivars of flowering raspberry: 'Albus' has white flowers; 'Pink-Flowered Thimbleberry' has pink flowers.

Salix discolor

Pussy willow

BLOOM TIME: late winter

HEIGHT/WIDTH: 10'–18' × 5'–8' (3–5.5 × 1.5–2.5m)

LIGHT: full sun

ZONES: 4–8

OTHER: catkins for cutting

Pussy willow

For many, the sight of pussy willow catkins announcing winter's close are the quintessence of childhood memories. The soft gray 2-inch (5cm) -long catkins on slender red-brown stems invite you to touch them, and look supremely artistic in a vase of any kind. *Salix discolor* has leaves that are colored blue-green on the undersides.

Native to North America, this pussy willow is generally found in the wild along streambanks and in wetlands. Easy enough to trim into small tree form, the deciduous pussy willow requires full sun and ample water. Otherwise, it is not fussy, adapting to any soil and even to poor drainage, so it's the perfect plant for that swampy spot. Be warned, however, that pest insects may visit, tree diseases can take hold, and a shallow, somewhat invasive rooting system deters underplanting. Pussy willow's hardy rooting system does have one advantage: it makes this fast-growing shrub excellent for erosion control.

Salvia leucantha

Mexican bush sage

BLOOM TIME: winter–spring

HEIGHT/WIDTH: 4' × 3' (1.2 × 1m)

LIGHT: full sun

ZONES: 10–11

OTHER: attracts hummingbirds, butterflies

Mexican bush sage

All the salvias seem to beckon to hummingbirds, and connoisseurs have entire gardens consisting of nothing but different types of salvias: shrub, subshrub, perennial, and annual. Mexican bush sage has long, velvety, rose-purple or lavender-purple spikes inset with small white flowers. There are also all-purple and all-pink varieties available from some specialty nurseries.

This sturdy salvia is native to Mexico and tropical Central America, and likes to stay on the slightly dry side once established. Like most herbs, Mexican bush sage demands a very sunny site and soil with excellent drainage. While blooms usually appear on the bush from winter to spring, in some growing areas flowers are seen throughout the year. Attractive, lance-shaped, grayish green leaves have the typical sage aroma when rubbed between the fingers.

Other shrub sages include autumn sage (*S. greggi*), purple sage (*S. leucophylla*), *S. microphylla*, *S. muelleri*, and *S. regla*.

Sambucus canadensis

American elderberry

BLOOM TIME: early summer

HEIGHT/WIDTH: 10' × 10' (3 × 3m)

LIGHT: full sun

ZONES: 4–9

OTHER: attracts birds

American elderberry

If you need a fast-growing, quick-spreading shrub and like the "wild" look (or are willing to prune regularly), this native North American might work well in your large garden. A truly rampant grower, American elderberry grows best in moist, well-drained, organic soil and full sun.

Creamy white, flat-topped flower clusters, about 8 inches (20cm) wide are followed by profuse clusters of fruits that are much enjoyed by birds. The purple-black fruits of selected forms of American elderberries are good baked in pies or made into jellies, and the really ambitious gardener can make old-time elderberry wine from the purple-black fruits. Two fruiting varieties are needed for pollination. No elderberry fruit should be eaten uncooked, and red fruits are never edible.

American elderberry can be left unpruned, or it can be pruned hard if you want to cut back its growth. Prune early in spring, while the bush is still dormant, so that the new growth can bear flowers and berries.

There is also another ornamental elderberry, called golden elder (*Sambucus canadensis* 'Aurea'), with bright yellow to yellow-green foliage.

Spiraea prunifolia

Bridal wreath

BLOOM TIME: midspring

HEIGHT/WIDTH: 6' × 8' (1.8 × 2.5m)

LIGHT: full sun

ZONES: 4–10

OTHER: attracts butterflies; good cutting branches

Bridal wreath

The arching bare branches of this deciduous shrub are covered in spring with rounded bouquets of small, white, double flowers, each resembling a tiny rose. Spirea is among the most popular of garden shrubs, and bridal wreath is at the top of the popularity poll. Other than the shrub's sheer beauty, gardeners list bridal wreath's very easy culture as the chief reason to grow it—truly an amateur's delight.

Spirea will thrive almost anywhere as long as it receives moderate water. It grows best in full sun but will tolerate some light shade. In addition to its lovely spring flowers, bridal wreath features handsome dark green leaves that turn orange or red in autumn.

Prune bridal wreath just after it flowers, as blooms are carried on the previous year's wood. In China, where this spirea has been a favorite garden plant for many hundreds of years, its name translates as "smile-laugh-flowers."

Symphoricarpos orbiculatus

Coralberry

BLOOM TIME: spring

HEIGHT/WIDTH: 5' × 4' (1.5 × 1.2m)

LIGHT: full sun–medium shade

ZONES: 2–9

OTHER: attracts honeybees, birds

'Variegatus' coralberry

Wind, poor soil, sites under trees, and pollution don't faze this aptly named native North American shrub. Dense and bushy, it sports dark coral-red, inedible, pea-sized fruit along bare stems in autumn and winter. Fruit may cause stomach upset or skin irritation. Racemes consisting of many small, pinkish green flowers precede berries.

Because deciduous coralberry is so cold-tolerant and tough, and tends to naturalize via suckers, this shrub makes a great bank and waterside cover where you have only natural rainfall, and it can be grown in the North. Woolly gray-green leaves may turn orange-red in autumn. Long ago, coralberry branches were used to make baskets.

'Variegatus Coralberry' is a potentially lower-growing, sun-only version, with leaves edged and veined in yellow. Note that many catalogs list the species *Symphoricarpos orbiculatus* as *S. vulgaris*, so if you can't find coralberry under the name listed above, try the synonym.

Syringa vulgaris

Common lilac

BLOOM TIME: late spring

HEIGHT/WIDTH: 12' × 10' (3.5 × 3m)

LIGHT: full sun

ZONES: 4–8

OTHER: attracts butterflies; cut flower; forcing indoors

Common lilac

Pioneers traveling westward purchased lilacs from plant peddlers and placed these nostalgic fragrant shrubs near the entrances of their new wilderness homes. In spring, lilacs are festooned with blossoms in shades of pink, blue, purple, mauve, and white. While lilac flowers symbolize modesty, the purple ones signify the romances of youth.

Grow lilacs in rich, moist, well-drained soil that is neutral or slightly alkaline. A sunny site is perfect, but hot, humid conditions are not tolerated. Deciduous common lilac can be trimmed into tree shape. Lilacs are often bothered by lilac scale and borers.

Common lilacs have been widely hybridized, most famously by the French nurseryman Victor Lemoine, and these hybrids are known as French lilacs. The individual names seem to span not only several countries, but several continents: 'Alphonse Lavallee', 'Congo', 'Jan van Tol' 'Charles X', 'Krasavitsa Moskvy', and 'Yankee Doodle'. There are more than fifty different types of French lilacs to choose from, all quite durable. Most fragrance lovers put several in the garden, choosing cultivars that bloom at different times to extend the season.

Vaccinium corymbosum

Highbush blueberry

BLOOM TIME: spring

HEIGHT/WIDTH: 6' × 8' (1.8 × 2.5m)

LIGHT: full sun

ZONES: 3–8

OTHER: attracts birds; edible berries

Highbush blueberry

If you can grow your own blueberries, do. Not only are the shrubs highly ornamental, but the freshly picked fruits are indescribably better than any found on the grocery produce shelf. Northern highbush blueberries require true winter cold, and ripen between June and August. For mild-winter areas, the newer Southern highbush blueberries ripen in April and May. There are multiple varieties available, and the best choice will depend on your growing area and particular tastes.

Blueberry flowers are tiny and whitish; the leaves are blue-green but with beautiful autumn color variation. All blueberries require cool, moist, well-drained, acidic soil.

They thrive in a soil with a pH of between 4.5 and 5.5, so if your soil is neutral or alkaline you may need to add an acidifier or to replace the soil around the shrub altogether.

Mulch the blueberries to conserve water and to protect fine roots that stay near the soil surface. Pruning is not usually necessary, but you may want to cut out old canes to improve flowering and berry production. You'll most likely want to plant several types, both for pollination advantages and to gain a long fruiting season. Birds love blueberries, so you may have to protect the tasty fruits with netting if you want a reasonable harvest.

Viburnum carlcephalum

Fragrant snowball

BLOOM TIME: spring

HEIGHT/WIDTH: 8' × 8' (2.5 × 2.5m)

LIGHT: full sun–partial shade

ZONES: 6–8

OTHER: attracts birds

Fragrant snowball

The bright red fruit of fragrant snowball, which ripen to black, act as a veritable magnet for birds. Small, waxy, white, tubular flowers are supremely fragrant, and they burst forth from pink buds into multiple 6-inch (15cm) -wide globular clusters. Heart-shaped, toothed leaves, 5 inches (13cm) wide, turn a lively reddish purple in autumn.

Fragrant snowball is a deciduous shrub with loose, open, wide-spreading branches. It looks best planted as a specimen, as its large flower clusters and spreading habit do not mix well in a shrub border.

Viburnums, as a group, prefer moist, well-drained, slightly acidic soil, although they can tolerate some deviation. Give them regular water and fertilizer for best flowering and general vigor. Fragrant snowball sometimes has trouble getting established after transplanting, but once the roots are established it is quite low maintenance. Fruiting improves if several viburnums of the same species are planted near each other so that cross-pollination can occur.

Viburnum plicatum var. tomentosum

Doublefile viburnum

BLOOM TIME: late spring–early summer

HEIGHT/WIDTH: 10' × 10' (3 × 3m)

LIGHT: full sun–partial shade

ZONES: 4–8

OTHER: good cutting branches

'Shoshoni' doublefile viburnum

A somewhat ordinary shrub when not in bloom, this doublefile viburnum's miniature bouquets are so gorgeous that they make it worth including in the garden. Tiers of horizontal branches are laden with deliciously fragrant white flower clusters, each 4 inches (10cm) wide. The clusters are carried above the foliage on either side of the branches, giving the shrub its common name "doublefile." Following the flowers are red fruits that usually ripen to black. Leaves, a yellow-green throughout most of the growing season, turn purple-red in autumn.

Deciduous viburnums tolerate a wide range of soil conditions, although they prefer moist, well-drained, organic soil and will not tolerate drought. You'll need to prune only dead wood; prune in early summer, after flowering. Viburnums will grow in either sun or partial shade, which makes them particularly versatile shrubs.

Cultivars include 'Japanese Snowball', 'Shasta Snowball', 'Shoshoni', and 'Summer Snowflake'. There's also a compact 'Pink Snowball', with fragrant flowers that open white, then fade to a deep pink.

Viburnum trilobum

American cranberry bush

BLOOM TIME: late spring

HEIGHT/WIDTH: 12' × 12' (3.5 × 3.5m)

LIGHT: full sun–partial shade

ZONES: 2–7

OTHER: attracts birds; berries for fruit jelly

American cranberry bush

Yellow and red fruits ripen to scarlet in late summer and persist through winter, that is, if the birds leave any leftovers. You might also want to rob the shrub of its fruit to make homemade cranberry jelly.

Small, pinwheel-shaped, pleasantly scented, white flowers cover American cranberry bush with 3-inch (7cm) bouquets in spring. The shrub's maplelike leaves turn flaming red in autumn.

This deciduous eastern North American native is particularly fond of moist soil rich in humus and lime. American cranberry bush does best in full sun but will tolerate some shade. Sited properly it is quite tough, although aphids may turn up for an occasional meal. Pruning isn't necessary except for the removal of dead branches. Planted in groups and allowed to grow to full size, American cranberry bushes make attractive shelter for birds.

In addition to the medium-height version, there's a smaller, 4-foot (1.2m) -tall cultivar, 'Compactum', which provides an excellent choice for small yards and patios.

Vitex agnus-castus

Chaste tree

BLOOM TIME: summer–autumn

HEIGHT/WIDTH: 10' × 12' (3 × 3.5m)

LIGHT: full sun

ZONES: 6–9

OTHER: attracts butterflies, honeybees

Chaste tree

This handsome shrub got its name from the alleged ability of its flowers and foliage to tame lust; it was widely planted in England in centuries past, presumably for this talent. Today not grown as often as it should be, this tolerant shrub is a fine addition to those often difficult seaside gardens, as well as other garden sections. Requiring little care, it prefers a medium-dry situation. Small, quite fragrant, lilac-blue flowers charm on 6- to 8-inch (15 to 20cm) panicles at branch ends, and last from late summer through autumn. Long narrow leaflets are gray-green above, gray beneath.

If you live in a warm climate, expect chaste tree to grow rapidly to 25 feet (7.5m) tall. But if you reside in a cooler climate, it may reach 10 feet (3m), and in even colder areas, grow to just 3 feet (1m) in height. This is because even relatively mild winters will cause dieback. Simply prune the dead branches to the ground; the shrub will grow back quickly, and since flowers are borne on the current season's growth, there is no loss of bloom. Protect newly planted chaste trees through their first winter by placing a cold frame over them. The cultivar 'Alba' has white flowers.

Weigela florida

Rose weigela, cardinal shrub

BLOOM TIME: late spring–early summer

HEIGHT/WIDTH: 6' × 6' (1.8 × 1.8m)

LIGHT: full sun–light shade

ZONES: 5–8

OTHER: attracts hummingbirds, birds; flowering branches good for arrangements

'Rubridor' rose weigela

Take your pick of foliage colors — red, brown-red, purple-green, green, green and white, gold, or yellow-green trimmed in red — when you go to select one or more of the modern cardinal shrub cultivars for your autumn-color garden. This practically pest-free, disease-resistant, and pollution-tolerant shrub is almost guaranteed to bring courting hummingbirds into your yard. Ample nectar comes from profuse, clustered, 1-inch (2.5cm) -wide tubular flowers colored rosy pink, crimson-red, wine red with golden centers, or dwarf lilac-purple with yellow center.

Give this shrub regular watering and well-drained soil, but it does tolerate nearly any soil type. Weigela will get quite large, so make sure to give it plenty of garden space. It grows best when sited in full sun, but will still thrive under light shade. Prune only lightly, to get rid of dead branches and to thin out canes.

Try the smaller weigela cultivars, 'Bristol Ruby' and 'Bristol Snowflake' for example, as potted plants for patio gardens. Some cultivars, such as 'Red Prince' and 'Evita', may even rebloom reliably.

Xanthorhiza simplicissima

Yellowroot

BLOOM TIME: spring

HEIGHT/WIDTH: 2'–3' × 3' (.6–1 × 1m)

LIGHT: partial shade–full shade

ZONES: 3–9

Yellowroot

This small deciduous shrub is grown primarily for its attractive 2- to 4-inch (5 to 10cm) -long, shiny green, deeply toothed leaves. The foliage turns a handsome bronze-purple in autumn, giving a long display. Inner bark is yellow, as are the roots. Small, purplish, grouped flowers are rather inconspicuous.

At an almost uniform 24 to 36 inches (60 to 90cm) tall, depending on location, a common alternate use for yellowroot is as a very cold-hardy, shrubby groundcover.

Yellowroot will spread rapidly by suckers, making large patches if given a wind-free, moist, mostly shady growing site. It is excellent for the areas beneath trees or for edging a shrub border, and can be a perfect solution for that damp, shady site where little else will grow. Often seen growing along streambanks, yellowroot is native to the wet woods of eastern North America.

PLANT HARDINESS ZONES

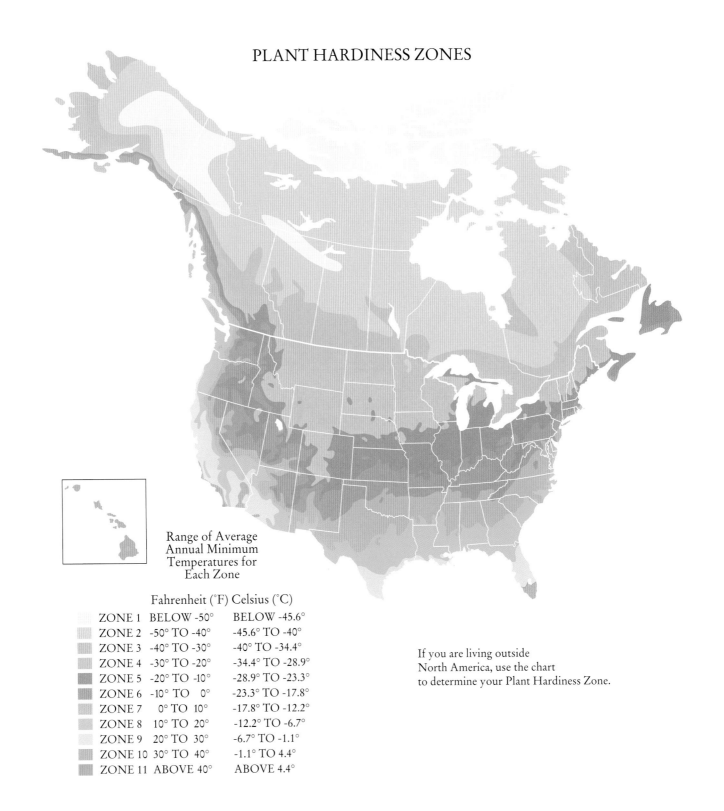

Range of Average
Annual Minimum
Temperatures for
Each Zone

Fahrenheit (˚F) Celsius (˚C)

		Fahrenheit (˚F)	Celsius (˚C)
	ZONE 1	BELOW -50°	BELOW -45.6°
	ZONE 2	-50° TO -40°	-45.6° TO -40°
	ZONE 3	-40° TO -30°	-40° TO -34.4°
	ZONE 4	-30° TO -20°	-34.4° TO -28.9°
	ZONE 5	-20° TO -10°	-28.9° TO -23.3°
	ZONE 6	-10° TO 0°	-23.3° TO -17.8°
	ZONE 7	0° TO 10°	-17.8° TO -12.2°
	ZONE 8	10° TO 20°	-12.2° TO -6.7°
	ZONE 9	20° TO 30°	-6.7° TO -1.1°
	ZONE 10	30° TO 40°	-1.1° TO 4.4°
	ZONE 11	ABOVE 40°	ABOVE 4.4°

If you are living outside
North America, use the chart
to determine your Plant Hardiness Zone.

Mail-Order Sources

Following are some excellent mail-order sources for shrubs. Many other catalogs may also include shrubs in their offerings, and local nurseries may prove good sources for interesting shrubs.

Canyon Creek Nursery
3527 Dry Creek Road
Oroville, CA 95965
530-533-2166

Eastern Plant Specialties
Box 226
Georgetown, ME 04548
207-371-2888
Catalog: $3.00

Forest Farm
990 Tetherow Road
Williams, OR 97544-9599
541-846-7269
Catalog: $4.00

High Country Gardens
2902 Rufina Street
Santa Fe, NM 87505-2929
505-438-3031

Klehm Nursery
4210 North Duncan Road
Champaign, IL 61821
217-373-8400
Catalog: $4.00

Musser Forests, Inc.
P.O. Box 340
Indiana, PA 15710
800-643-8319

Northwoods Nursery
27635 S. Oglesby Road
Canby, OR 97013
503-266-5432

Oikos Tree Crops
P.O. Box 19425
Kalamazoo, MI 49019
616-624-6233

Raintree Nursery
391 Butts Road
Morton, WA 98356
360-496-6400

Wayside Gardens
1 Garden Lane
Hodges, SC 29695-0001
800-845-1124

Weiss Brothers Nursery
11690 Colfax Highway
Grass Valley, CA 95945
916-272-7657

Australian Sources

Country Farm Perennials
RSD Laings Road
Nayook VIC 3821

Cox's Nursery
RMB 216 Oaks Road
Thrilmere NSW 2572

Honeysuckle Cottage Nursery
Lot 35 Bowen Mountain Road
Bowen Mountain via Grosevale
NSW 2753

Swan Bros Pty Ltd
490 Galston Road
Dural NSW 2158

Canadian Sources

Corn Hill Nursery Ltd.
RR 5
Petitcodiac NB EOA 2HO

Ferncliff Gardens
SS 1
Mission, British Columbia
V2V 5V6

McFayden Seed Co. Ltd.
Box 1800
Brandon, Manitoba
R7A 6N4

Stirling Perennials
RR 1
Morpeth, Ontario
N0P 1X0

Further Reading

Azaleas, Rhododendrons & Camellias
Sunset Editors
Sunset Publishing Co., 1982

Diseases of Trees and Shrubs
Wayne A. Sinclair, Howard H.
Lyon, and Warren T. Johnson
Cornell University Press, 1987

*Flowering Shrubs: Step-by-Step to
Growing Success*
David Carr
Crowood Press, 1992

Flowering Shrubs and Small Trees
Isabel Zucker; revised by
Derek Fell
Friedman/Fairfax Publishers,
1995

*Gardening with Roses: Designing with
Easy-Care Climbers, Ramblers, and
Shrubs*
Judith C. McKeon
Friedman/Fairfax Publishers,
1997

*Pruning Made Easy: A Gardener's
Visual Guide to When and How to
Prune Everything, from Flowers
to Trees*
Lewis Hill and Elayne Sears
Storey Books, 1998

Shrub Identification Book
A.W. Merwin and George W.
Symonds
William Morrow & Co., 1973